PRAISE FOR

THE END OF REJECTION

The proven balance, practical wisdom and spiritual sensitivity demonstrated by Chris Hayward is helping an increasing number of leaders to shape workers for the demanding task of helping others find freedom from long-ensconced, growth-inhibiting strongholds in their lives. Here is another tool to contribute to the cleansing and equipping of saints "without spot or wrinkle . . . or any other blemish."

Jack W. Hayford
President, The International Foursquare Church

Rejection steps over all boundaries in its search to work its damage. Now a book arrives that deals with this common struggle and uses clear-cut truths to bring lasting freedom!

Jim Tolle
Senior Pastor, The Church On The Way

Rejection afflicts about as many people spiritually and emotionally as the common cold afflicts people physically. There is no cure for the common cold, but there is for rejection. In this uplifting book, Chris Hayward diagnoses rejection and then leads you personally, step by step, through effective treatment. Read it, and your door to the freedom you desire will be opened once and for all!

C. Peter Wagner
Chancellor, Wagner Leadership Institute

CHRIS HAYWARD

THE END
OF REJECTION

YOUR PAST
IS NOT YOUR
FUTURE

Regal

From Gospel Light
Ventura, California, U.S.A.

PUBLISHED BY REGAL BOOKS
FROM GOSPEL LIGHT
VENTURA, CALIFORNIA, U.S.A.
PRINTED IN THE U.S.A.

Regal Books is a ministry of Gospel Light, a Christian publisher dedicated to serving the local church. We believe God's vision for Gospel Light is to provide church leaders with biblical, user-friendly materials that will help them evangelize, disciple and minister to children, youth and families.

It is our prayer that this Regal book will help you discover biblical truth for your own life and help you meet the needs of others. May God richly bless you.

For a free catalog of resources from Regal Books/Gospel Light, please call your Christian supplier or contact us at 1-800-4-GOSPEL or www.regalbooks.com.

Library of Congress Cataloging-in-Publication Data
Hayward, Chris, 1946-
   The end of rejection / Chris Hayward.
      p. cm.
   ISBN 0-8307-4317-0 (trade paper)
   1. Rejection (Psychology)—Religious aspects—Christianity. 2. Salvation. I. Title.
   BV4905.3.H395 2007
   234—dc22   2006029149

   2   3   4   5   6   7   8   9   10   /   10   09   08   07

Rights for publishing this book in other languages are contracted by Gospel Light Worldwide, the international nonprofit ministry of Gospel Light. Gospel Light Worldwide also provides publishing and technical assistance to international publishers dedicated to producing Sunday School and Vacation Bible School curricula and books in the languages of the world. For additional information, visit www.gospel lightworldwide.org; write to Gospel Light Worldwide, P.O. Box 3875, Ventura, CA 93006; or send an e-mail to info@gospellightworldwide.org.

*To my friend and wife, Karen, who has only
and ever shown me love.*

CONTENTS

Part One: Prologue

A View from the Garden
Adam and Eve moved in step with each other without shame, without fear—walking together in the contented gratitude that wholeness and holiness bring. What they could not see was heaven's Great War. Lucifer's last stand was about to take place.

The Great Seduction
Somewhere in time—before the weight of sin caused all creation to groan—the one known only as "serpent" began to speak . . . and Eve listened. Pride and unbelief had entered the Garden, and Lucifer was pleased.

The Beginning of Shame
Adam and Eve had never sinned until now. They never knew shame until now. These frightening and foreign feelings were, they supposed, somehow connected with death. It would be a long time before their agony and tears would go away.

Part Two: The Knowledge of Good and Evil

More Than a Tree
If people are convinced that they are children of God and have received His righteousness through Jesus Christ, they will be motivated to act accordingly. If, though they are God's children, they believe they are dirty, rotten sinners, then they will most likely act as such.

Getting a Foothold

The spirit of rejection can gain a foothold through a personal trauma; it can also gain a foothold through generational iniquity—a bent toward a particular sin—that, if left unrepented, is passed on from one generation to the next.

God Wants You Free!

Rejection is the act of denying love to someone; it is antithetical to God's nature, for God Himself is love, and because of His great love, He sent His Son to die so that those who had rejected God's love could be restored to Him.

Part Three: Walls in the Garden

The Rejection of God

All rejection begins with a rejection of God. Adam and Eve rejected God—His Word, His ways, and His love. When they did, they opened the door to the spirit of rejection. So it is for us. When we reject God, we become subject to rejection.

Self-Rejection

When confronted with shame, we can allow the Lord to deal with it or we can try to cover it ourselves. The root of self-rejection and self-hatred is shame; but often that shame is false, though its results are tragically real.

Fear of Rejection

One of the main objectives of our adversary is to convince us that God is not good—and not safe—for then we will be afraid to face Him and will do almost anything to avoid Him. But God comes to us where we are—in our hiding place.

Rejection of Others
When we find it impossible to rid ourselves of rejection, someone else usually pays. By blaming, faultfinding, and pointing a finger at others, we are able to mask how terrible we feel on the inside and place our misery on others. In essence, we reject them.

Part Four: Epilogue

The Clothing of God
With His hands, God killed, gutted and skinned the lamb; and with the skins still warm from the blood that once flowed, He removed their fig leaves and covered Adam and Eve with the skin of the lamb—clothing them with God-given innocence.

Evidence of Grace
In that last face-to-face Eden conversation, God gave Adam and Eve a promise that someday a Savior would come to crush the head of the adversary. In fact, He clothed them with the reminder that another sacrifice would one day be made.

ACKNOWLEDGMENTS

The enjoyment of working on this book has been that of collaborating with some very special people.

Ron and Carol Morris, thank you for providing a most beautiful place for me to hibernate, pray and collect my thoughts for a few days. Your home was the launching pad for this book.

Christi Goeser, you blessed me more than you realize. Your gracious encouragement while looking over my "first draft" kept me moving along, believing there was something worthwhile to be said on this subject.

Kathi Macias, thank you for your practical and spiritual insights. They, as well as your recognized editorial skill, have been invaluable.

Karen, you of all people have brought such wonderful understanding of acceptance into my life. Through 35 years of marriage, you have been totally supportive and encouraging. You have taught me what rejection is not.

PART ONE

PROLOGUE

A VIEW FROM THE GARDEN

God saw all that he had made, and it was very good.

GENESIS 1:31

Life was perfect—quite perfect in fact. The land was alive with a powerful beauty that filled their souls and left them breathless at the same time. Harmony. Grace. Strength. All around and within echoed a ceaseless cry of wonder and worship. Their lives were mysteriously knit together in sacred link. They moved in step with each other without shame, without fear—walking together in the contented gratitude that wholeness and holiness bring. There was nothing to worry about, no cares to weigh them down. It was idyllic.

There were no questions about God, no doubts about their relationship with Him. They conversed with Him daily. They knew they were loved, and they simply and innocently loved in return.

What they could not see was heaven's Great War. Lucifer's last stand was about to take place. An angelic being of great power and importance, his pride and arrogance, now revealed, would result in a clash of monumental—even universal—proportions. Ten thousands of ten thousands would enter into the conflict. Along with Lucifer, a third of these angels would be cast out of heaven under his maniacal leadership. This great

war of angels—their campaigns and strategies, wins and losses—
would never be chronicled in the libraries of man, but its influence would spill over to the earth in continued rebellion.

Could it be that Lucifer requested Earth as the place for his
ongoing war? Perhaps. Maybe the father of lies saw an opportunity to challenge and conquer the Almighty in a uniquely personal way. In Lucifer's twisted mind, the weak and infuriating
beings known as Adam and Eve—less than angels but loved by
God—could be his ticket to justification. For if this newly created, perfect race would rebel against God, then how could angels
be judged for doing the same?

Pride blinds. Somewhere in all of his grand plans, Lucifer
disregarded the fact that God is eternal. His feet stand in both
the past and the future with equal ease; His wisdom and power
are without limit.

Earth would indeed be the new battleground—not by Lucifer's choice but by God's sovereign decree. And the theme for this
final stand would be redemption—a fitting objective in Lucifer's
mind, considering that God had rejected his claim to equality.
If humankind, being perfect, would reject God's sovereign rule,
then how could Lucifer be blamed for doing the same? He could,
instead, be redeemed and restored to his rightful place, while
God would be humbled and seen as unjust, unfair and weak.

So it was that Earth, the perfect world of radiant beauty,
became the great theater of proof. In the end, Lucifer thought
that he could still win. Then, not only would he be restored to his
rightful place, but he would also be recognized in his newly exalt-
ed position—equal to God Himself. After all, Lucifer once roamed
the hallowed halls of heaven, coming unannounced before the

throne. We might infer from the words of Job 1 that he had an audience with God whenever he pleased. None in heaven possessed his beauty, grace and abilities; none could compare to him—least of all this new race created "in the image of God." Lucifer, in all his beauty and self-importance, would not be put aside by these puny, earthly creatures. They were loved by God, and as such were a threat that must be removed at all costs. It would truly be poetic justice. Humanity would fall. God would be rejected. Lucifer would be justified. And heaven would be brought under his rulership.

Pride blinds. This arrogant usurper of heaven's throne failed to see the greater Plan, formed before creation, agreed upon by the eternal Godhead. According to God's providence, power would be overthrown by weakness; pride subdued by humility; hatred defeated by love; and greatness revealed by servanthood.

The Savior was coming!

Making It Personal

1. Describe the closest you've ever come to feeling as if you were in an idyllic situation—the next best thing to heaven itself. What do you think it was about that situation that made you feel that way?

2. Name the relationships you have now (or had in the past) in which you never doubted that you were loved. How did you feel? How did it affect your view of yourself? If you have never experienced that sort of relationship, how do you think your life might have been different if you had?

THE GREAT SEDUCTION

*And the LORD God commanded the man, "You are free to eat from
any tree in the garden; but you must not eat from the tree of the knowledge
of good and evil, for when you eat of it you will surely die."*

GENESIS 2:16-17

Somewhere in time it began. The one known only as "serpent" began to speak. To Eve, it was not a strange thing. Perhaps there was a time when creatures spoke, before the weight of sin caused all creation to groan.

We do not know how long this particular conversation endured. It might have been weeks, or even months. Lucifer himself occupied this subtle and crafty creature, and time was on his side. Through patience and stealth he would turn this idyllic garden into a place of agony.

Eve was brilliant and beautiful, perfect in every way, but naïve. She knew nothing of guile. The term "truth" was nonexistent. To understand truth, there would also need to be a comprehension of lies, and with this she had no such acquaintance.

It was a time when love reigned supreme. There was no suspicion, no doubt, no deception and no defensiveness—only trust. In such an atmosphere of childlike trust, the serpent was believed.

"Did God really say . . . ?" This one simple question, these four words, contained the insidious poison that would begin to pollute the human race. There had never before been a question of God's intentions—this one question contained the DNA that would assail the very character of God, which was precisely Lucifer's intention: assail the character of God, remove any sense of trust, call into question His intentions, and victory would be virtually assured.

Eve had never questioned God. There was never any reason to do so. But now the serpent was planting the poison of *doubt* in her mind: Why would God withhold knowledge from her? What was there about this tree that He wouldn't want her to know? Was knowing about good and evil wrong? What *was* evil? There was something terribly intriguing about all this. A tree with fruit, not unlike other trees in the Garden, yet now with this restriction it seemed so appealing.

And why was God so silent about all this? He had offered no further explanation other than proclaiming the restriction. At least the serpent reasoned with her. God's silence must surely mean that He could not deny the serpent's claim. God was holding back; He was denying Eve something of value. He would not do this unless she was of less value than the fruit being withheld. Perhaps she was not as valuable to God as she first thought. Perhaps He had rejected her. Yes, that was it—God had rejected her.

And why was Adam so quiet about all this? He saw; he listened; he said nothing.

Eve took hold of the fruit and ate it. Then she handed it to her husband who was standing there, an eyewitness to it all. Why didn't he prevent this awful tragedy?

Adam also had never been lied to. He knew that what was being said didn't resonate with the word spoken by God. God had said they must not eat of the tree. But why did Eve say they also should not touch it? Touching and eating were altogether different. So the serpent was somewhat correct; God didn't say they would die if they touched it. Confusion began to set in.

There was another factor playing into all of this. Adam had waited so long for Eve. Although he loved God, it was Eve who completed him. Every day with her was an adventure. There was no pleasure as exhilarating as her affection for him. He sought only to please her, to discover the world through her eyes. He had never resisted her; there had never been a reason to do so. Why would he resist her now? What would happen if he did? How would she respond? Would her affection for him change? For the first time in his life he experienced the emotion of fear.

For Eve, the feeling was rejection. She loved Adam and had never withheld anything from him. So if God loved her, why would He withhold anything from her? There was only one answer: Her Lord, her God, had rejected her.

Adam's fear was fully realized when Eve took the fruit and ate. He knew the result of breaking the command: "You will surely die." Now she was offering the fruit to him. What should he do? He had never experienced death. He knew only that unless he joined Eve in her mutinous act, he would surely lose her. She would be taken from him, and he could not bear the thought. If she had to die, then he would die with her. Whatever was to happen to her would happen to him. Yes, Adam knew exactly what he was doing.

In time another Adam would be born. He too could not bear the thought of losing *His* Bride. He also would die. The first Adam's fear of losing blinded him to the obvious—that perhaps God would allow him to die in her place. Then *she* could live. He failed to see that in trying to save his own life, he lost it. Pride and unbelief had entered the Garden. Adam and Eve had both succumbed to its charm . . . and Lucifer was pleased.

Making It Personal

1. Consider a time when you were drawn into making a decision that you knew you should avoid. Why do you suppose this happened?

2. When have you ignored a warning and, like Eve, taken matters into your own hands? What were the far-reaching effects?

THE BEGINNING OF SHAME

*Then the man and his wife heard the sound of the LORD God
as he was walking in the garden in the cool of the day, and they hid
from the LORD God among the trees of the garden.*

GENESIS 3:8

As the evening began to cool, a light breeze stirred the leaves. It was the time when God came to walk with those made in His image—a time of closeness, a time of intimacy. These times together with God were warm and wonderful for the first man and woman. They were moments of discovery and joy, and every evening Adam and Eve looked forward to their Creator's delightful questions:

- "What did you discover today, My children?"
- "Have you thought about the dimensions of the earth, and what supports its foundations?"
- "Have you ever wondered how I command the morning to appear and cause the dawn to rise in the east?"
- "Do you realize the extent of the earth?"
- "Tell me what you know."
- "Where does the light come from, and where does the darkness go?"

They loved His playful ways with them and His probing questions. Every evening was different. Mysteries unfolded, and they were enlightened by His very presence.

But tonight—tonight was different. The gentle cool of the evening had given way to the biting cold of fear. They were no longer comfortable. The rustling of the leaves in the trees stirred their sense of foreboding. Now, instead of looking forward to God's presence, they wanted to run from Him. Worst of all, there seemed to be a new voice in their heads. Chiming in with their sense of failure, it said, *All is lost. Things will never be the same. There is no hope, and joy will never return.*

Pain of the Fall

How to describe the ache in the pit in their stomachs, the dazed heaviness deep in their hearts? And then there was the thirst—a spiritual thirst. At first, they thought a deep drink from the clear pool of spring water could quench it. But as they stooped to drink, they saw their own reflections, and for the first time they quickly drew back. For the first time, they didn't like what they saw. When they had first been created, they had seen God's smile and heard the words, "This is good." Now, what God had once said was good no longer looked good to them.

The usually playful animals froze in place as they heard a sound foreign to their ears. Although they knew Adam's voice and it had always been a comfort to them, tonight they did not recognize it. Never had they heard such a sound! It was the sound of an agonizing moan. Anguished and full of regret, Adam could be seen clenching his fists and beating them against his chest. And there, just a few feet away, Eve rocked mournfully on her knees, her eyes full of tears and her face cupped in her hands.

Shame

Neither of them fully understood why they did these things, though in time they would. They had never sinned—until now. They had never known shame—until now. These frightening and foreign feelings were, they supposed, somehow connected with death. It would be a long time before their agony and tears would go away.

Later, Adam and Eve's children would attempt to mask the pain, using any number of diversions. But like an unrelenting weed, pain would inevitably spring up, taking on a new shape. Over time, other words came to describe their response to pain— "shame," "disgrace," "embarrassment," "dishonor," "humiliation" and "regret." Each descriptive but deceptive word was a new poison administered to the heart.

And there was always that incessant *other* voice in their heads, saying, "You are worthless and evil. Look at yourself: there is nothing beautiful or handsome about you. You are flawed and sick. The favor of God has left you. You'll have to prove your worth to Him from now on. You are self-centered and pathetic. You might as well give up. Things will never change. It would be better if you had never been created. You are a mistake. God regrets having made you. End it now and be done with it. If you do, the pain will stop."

Guilt

Another word—"guilt"—also found its way into the human vocabulary. Adam and Eve's descendants would come to realize that disobedience to God brought about an immediate sense of failure and shortcoming. This guilt came as a result of violating a command of God. In and of itself, the guilt was good, for it brought immediate realization that they had crossed the line and ventured into disobedience. This realization of the violation of God's command became known as *conscience*.

Humankind coped with the pain using more than just diversions; many chose to alter their thinking. They reasoned that if shame came as a result of guilt, and guilt came from violating one of God's commandments, then the answer was to get rid of God. Without God, there would be no guilt; without guilt, there would be no shame. Shame, therefore, could be eliminated. For some this worked, and they held fast to the notion that God did not exist. Many, however, could not hold up under the strain. They soon came to the conclusion that ending their life would stop the pain.

Condemnation

But what of those who clung to belief in God—who could not deny Him? To them the voice would say, "You have failed, and all is lost. God will never take you back. Your situation is hopeless. You are evil and no good. You are condemned forever." They called this feeling *condemnation*. After a while, some tried to convince them that this other voice was just a guilty conscience that stemmed from believing in God. Others tried to tell them that they weren't that bad. And still others said it was all in their heads.

What they failed to see was that the serpent, Lucifer, was purposefully moving amongst humankind as part of his plan to overthrow God. He had been busy giving assignments to the fallen angels who had gone down in defeat with him during heaven's Great War. A war was still being waged—though humankind was largely unaware of it. Lucifer reasoned that since the ploy had worked with Adam and Eve, it would work with their children as well. Lucifer, being limited, needed an army of soldiers to assist him in this devilish work, and there were plenty to go around. Their thinking was like Lucifer's thinking, and they acted in compliance with his mission: Man must fall; God must be rejected, Lucifer justified, and heaven brought under his rulership.

A Garden Without Walls

Eden was a garden without walls. The blessings of God were boundless. The freedom and joy that Adam and Eve experienced were exceeded only by the intimacy both had with God. His loving presence filled their hearts. But everything changed on that fateful day of rebellion. How could everything change so quickly? How could there be such joy one moment and such pain the next? How could eating a piece of seemingly insignificant fruit bring about such devastation? It may have taken a while for them to sort things out, but eventually it came to them.

The real issue had nothing to do with the tree or the fruit. The real issue was the command: "And the LORD God commanded the man, 'You are free to eat from any tree in the garden; but you must not eat from the tree of the knowledge of good and evil, for when you eat of it you will surely die'" (Gen. 2:16-17).

What made this fruit different from all others was the restriction. The serpent's ploy had worked. By introducing doubt, questioning motives and gradually assassinating the character of God, the desired result was assured.

The serpent was quite cunning in his question: "Did God really say, 'You must not eat from any tree in the garden'?" (3:1). In other words, "Do you know what you're talking about, Eve? Could you have misunderstood Him? If you truly love someone, would you restrict that loved one from pleasure?" Then came the final argument: "'You will not surely die,' the serpent said to the woman. 'For God knows that when you eat of it your eyes will be opened, and you will be like God, knowing good and evil'" (vv. 4-5). This was the beginning of pride and unbelief—unbelief in God's Word as the absolute truth, and pride in believing they deserved more than God had allotted them.

The insinuation was clear:

- "God is not telling you everything you need to know. You can't see clearly. Things are being hidden from you. God is holding out on you, and He doesn't want you to have good things."
- "You had better take care of yourself, Eve, and take matters into your own hands—or you will lose out."
- "Don't let this good thing get away from you."

These, and words like them, would be uttered to Adam and Eve's children many times over in the thousands of years that followed. The story rarely changes—neither does the choice of words. Why? Because the ploy works. If you introduce doubt and suspicion into a relationship, and if you begin to see yourself as more important than you are, regretful actions are the inevitable result. And the by-product is rejection—the first negative emotion to be experienced by the human race.

Rejection is at the core of every malady. It is the sinister spirit behind every sin. It is the motivating force behind all fear and hatred. It is at the center of every act of abuse and heartache ever endured by humankind. It has torn apart families, churches, cities and countries. And it is why the God of the universe committed Himself irreversibly to bring an end to it—the end of rejection.

The father of pride—Satan himself, and, therefore, the promoter of rejection—occupied the serpent, weaving his maniacal and deceptive web as he lured Eve into taking the forbidden fruit. His tactics to entrap humankind have not changed. The kingdom of darkness, now under his control, still perpetuates the deception.

Making It Personal

1. Think of your worst personal experience of betrayal. How did you feel the next time you saw the other person who was involved?

2. How have you or the other person tried to "get rid of [ignore] God" as a means of justifying the previous decision and/or behavior?

PART TWO

THE KNOWLEDGE OF
GOOD AND EVIL

MORE THAN A TREE

But of the tree of the knowledge of good and evil, thou shalt not eat of it:
for in the day that thou eatest thereof thou shalt surely die.
GENESIS 2:17, *KJV*

Throughout Part 1: Prologue, I attempted to bring some understanding to a certain aspect of the very familiar story of the Fall. What must it have been like to live before there was a sense of shame, guilt and confusion—to walk with Love and to live in His glory daily?

It is impossible to know with certainty how Adam and Eve felt or what they thought, but one thing is sure: They lived in complete freedom and perfect love. To fall from that life into one characterized by fear and distrust is incomprehensible to us because we have known nothing else. We live in a world infected by their sin, and we live in a world dominated by that rejection. As a result, all of our lives we have been affected. The good news is that God knew what would happen—that humankind would fall into sin—and had already provided a way for us to experience wholeness and restoration.

That's what this book is all about: seeing people who have been waylaid by sin and rejection restored to their God-intended destiny. We will return to the narrative in the epilogue. For now, let us leave the Garden and discuss the ways in which we can overcome the spirit of rejection.

Defining Terms

For us to truly understand what is meant by the term "the spirit of rejection," we need to look at the several ways the Bible refers to the word "spirit." In both Hebrew and Greek, the original languages of the Bible, the word "spirit" conveys the idea of breath or wind. Though intangible, spirit is real and has an effect on the physical world. This simple understanding of spirit blossoms into some very different meanings, depending on context. It might refer to the Spirit of God, to the human spirit or to an evil entity.

The Holy Spirit

"Nevertheless I tell you the truth. It is to your advantage that I go away; for if I do not go away, the Helper will not come to you; but if I depart, I will send Him to you. And when He has come, He will convict the world of sin, and of righteousness, and of judgment" (John 16:7-8, *NKJV*).

Conviction of sin. It is the work of the Holy Spirit to convict people of sin, and to convince them that they need a savior. It was the Holy Spirit that first made people aware of sin. When God convicts, it is obvious. He alerts with decisive clarity that the line between obedience and disobedience has been crossed. His conviction, however, always comes with an invitation to get things right—to repent and turn away from that sin and return to God.

Conviction of righteousness. It is also His continuing work to convict people of righteousness. What an interesting way to put it: *convict people of righteousness.* People don't often think of the Holy Spirit pointing His finger at them and saying, "You are righteous!" Yet that is exactly what He does in order to counteract the work of the adversary, the devil, who infects the children of God with lies, whispering about their "hopeless situation" and their "disgusting appearance before God." The Bible says, "For He made Him who knew no sin to be sin for us, that we might become the righteousness of God in Him" (2 Cor. 5:21, *NKJV*).

People often behave on the basis of what they perceive themselves to be. If they are convinced they are children of God and have received His righteousness through Jesus Christ, they will be motivated to act accordingly. However, if, though God's children, they believe they are dirty, rotten sinners, then they will most likely act as such.

Several years ago, a young Southern California couple adopted an eight-year-old girl from China. This child had spent the majority of her life in an orphanage, watching other younger children chosen for adoption while she stayed behind. Though it was explained to her before leaving the orphanage that she too had been adopted and was going to live with her new family in America, she seemed unable to grasp that truth. As a result, she spent the first few months in her new home fearing that at any moment she would be rejected and returned to the orphanage. She walked around with her eyes downcast, sat at the table without picking up a fork or spoon until her parents insisted she eat, and refused to show any emotion, regardless of the situation.

Because she felt that her status in the home was very tenuous, she even went so far as to slip out from between the sheets after her parents had tucked her in and then sleep on the throw rug next to her bed. The language barrier prevented the parents from communicating effectively with their new daughter, and so they had no idea why she exhibited such strange behavior, no matter how hard they tried to show their love and acceptance.

Then one day, as her English skills improved, the lonely little girl asked her language tutor to explain the word "daughter," for that was what her parents sometimes called her. She thought maybe it was the English equivalent of her Chinese name, which they also used in reference to her. When the tutor explained that the word "daughter" meant a girl child, she said that didn't describe her because she wasn't born to her American parents. The tutor then explained the word "adoption," telling the little girl that though she hadn't been physically born to her parents, she had been chosen by them out of all the children in the world to be their very own. As the impact of the tutor's explanation began to sink in, the little girl felt her fear melt away, and she realized she was there to stay and would not be sent back to the orphanage. She then ran from the room straight into the arms of her startled but very happy mother. The truth of her parents' unconditional love had dispelled her fear of rejection.

Conviction of judgment. The Holy Spirit also convicts people of judgment, for God's justice demands that both sin and sinners be judged. This is seen on several levels. Some of that judgment comes through natural consequences. For example, if someone chooses to live the life of an addict, then, as with all addictions, there is a price to pay. That judgment might come through God's allowing difficult tests and trials into the person's life designed to point that person toward repentance. Judgment might also come by some human instrument of affliction such as one person's working to oppose the actions of another. Judgment might ultimately come before the judgment seat of Christ where everyone will give an account of his or her life on Earth.

Yet, there is another judgment that often goes unnoticed. We are told about this as God pronounced judgment upon the serpent in the Garden of Eden:

> So the LORD God said to the serpent, "Because you have done this, Cursed are you above all the livestock and all the wild animals! You will crawl on your belly and you will eat dust all the days of your life. And I will put enmity between you and the woman, and between your offspring and hers; *he will crush your head, and you will strike his heel*" (Gen. 3:14-15, emphasis added).

In this one short statement, "he will crush your head and you will strike his heel," was revealed the plan of the ages. When the fullness of time had come, Jesus was born to a virgin, lived a life of perfection, showed us the heart of the Father, was falsely accused and died upon the cross where He took upon Himself all our sin and shame; then He rose victoriously from the grave. In that one fateful moment, what the enemy had thought was his victory became his defeat. Through the cross of Calvary, Satan "struck Jesus' heel." And when Jesus Christ rose from the grave, conquering death for all humankind, He "crushed" Satan's head. This phrase means that Satan's authority and power have been stripped away: "And having disarmed the powers and authorities, he made a public spectacle of them, triumphing over them by the cross" (Col. 2:15).

The Holy Spirit wants us to be convinced of the fact that our adversary, the devil, has been judged at the cross. Victory is assured. Though there will be many battles, God has already written the end of the story. Jesus Christ is triumphant, and His children are at His right hand, seated in heavenly places, coheirs with Him. So when facing this adversary, we must not grow weary but continue to fight the good fight: "[E]ven when we were dead in trespasses, [He] made us alive together with Christ (by grace you have been saved), and raised us up together, and made us sit together in the heavenly places in Christ Jesus" (Eph. 2:5-6).

I encourage you to study God's Word, as well as other books on the subject of the Holy Spirit, so that you can better understand the wonderful work of God's Spirit and His purpose toward us as the children of God. So much has been written about Him—and I could never do justice to Him in this brief section.

The Human Spirit

"And the very God of peace sanctify you wholly; and I pray God your whole spirit and soul and body be preserved blameless unto the coming of our Lord Jesus Christ" (1 Thess. 5:23, *KJV*).

Each person has been created as spirit, soul and body. Take any of these away and we cease to be human or alive on this earth. Why? Each part has an essential function.

First, and most obvious, we each have a body. For the child of God, to be absent from the body is to be present with the Lord (see 2 Cor. 5:8). This promise offers great hope and assurance to us as our body deteriorates over time, whether through old age or through sickness. (I believe in healing; however, the death rate among us is still one for one!)

Second, we each have a soul. It is in the realm of our soul that we have emotions and feelings:

Why are you downcast, O my soul? Why so disturbed within me? Put your hope in God, for I will yet praise him, my Savior and my God (Ps. 42:11).

Our soul is also the place of intellectual thought. We reason and make assessments in our mind, and our mind is influenced by reason and emotion.

You and I also have a spirit: "The spirit of a man is the lamp of the LORD, searching all the inner depths of his heart" (Prov. 20:27, NKJV). It is our spirits that are in communication with God. Our spirits are meant to have influence over our minds and emotions. Yes, the ability to reason is crucial, but it sometimes opposes what the Word of God declares and what faith requires. In the same way, our emotions are also important, but our emotions should never rule our actions. Rather, they should drive us to know the truth and to walk in it. They should give color and passion to our walk in Christ. They should display the love and compassion of Christ through our lives—but they should never govern our decisions.

Our spirit, before salvation in Christ, was dead because sin had brought death to it: "You were dead because of your sins and because your sinful nature was not yet cut away. Then God made you alive with Christ. He forgave all our sins" (Col. 2:13, NLT).

We know we were each walking around before we received Jesus as Savior. So what was dead? We could feel, we could think, we could make decisions—so what was dead? Our spirits had been brought to death through sin. From the time of Adam and Eve's fall, each subsequent generation was born spiritually dead. It is only through being "born again" through Jesus Christ that our spirit comes alive—*made alive with Christ*. It is through our spirit—that perfect part of ourselves, that part of ourselves that is in every way Christlike—that we have true communion with God, "who *delivered* us from so great a death, and *does deliver* us; in whom we trust that He *will still deliver* us" (2 Cor. 1:10, emphasis added).

- We *were delivered* the moment we expressed our faith in Jesus Christ (our spirit).
- We continue to be formed and molded into the image of Christ through sanctification, and so He *does deliver* us (our soul).
- Some day you and I will receive a glorified body at His appearance, and so He *will still deliver* us (our body).

However simple we attempt to make the functions of spirit, soul and body, it remains true that they are humanly indistinguishable. I cannot look at you and say, "Oh, there, I can see your soul, and here is your spirit." It takes the power of the Word of God to do such things: "For the word of God is living and active. Sharper than any double-edged sword, it penetrates even to *dividing soul and spirit*, joints and marrow; it judges the thoughts and attitudes of the heart" (Heb. 4:12, emphasis added).

It requires spiritual discernment to know what is of the soul and what is of the spirit. The Holy Spirit communes primarily with our spirit: "The Spirit Himself bears witness with our spirit that we are children of God" (Rom. 8:16, *NKJV*).

I was an assistant pastor in Texas when a college student told me of his desire to do something about the pornography that was rampant in his college. He was a young believer, and I discerned that he would be getting in over his head. I questioned him and his motives for doing this. He said all the right words that were consistent with Scripture, and so I told him to be sure to speak with me if he was getting into trouble. He assured me that he would be fine. Two months later, he came to my office in tears, confessing that he had fallen into the very thing he was fighting. It is possible to attempt good things out of our soul (mind, emotions and will), rather than being led by the Spirit of God through our spirit: "These things we also speak, not in words which man's wisdom teaches but which the Holy Spirit teaches, comparing spiritual things with spiritual. But the natural man does not receive the things of the Spirit of God, for they are foolishness to him; nor can he know them, because they are spiritually discerned" (1 Cor. 2:13-14).

We must all learn to be led by the Spirit and be able to discern between soulish things and spiritual matters. We have an amazing capacity to rationalize our behavior rather than being in tune with the Spirit of God.

Evil Spirits

For some time, I struggled with the idea of naming evil spirits— especially when I didn't see that name mentioned in the Word of

God. Were people just making things up? Were they just imagining that there was such a thing as an evil spirit? The devil would like us to believe that evil spirits exist only in our mind, that we are playing mind games with ourselves and others. The truth is that we should be cautious about pursuing any course of action if it cannot be substantiated in the Word of God.

We have an excellent example of this in the Gospels. In Mark 9, a father approached Jesus to explain to Him that his son was plagued with a mute spirit. The man had asked the disciples to cast it out of the boy, but they were unable to do so. Jesus rebuked the unclean spirit by its function: "When Jesus saw that the people came running together, He rebuked the unclean spirit, saying to it, 'Deaf and dumb spirit, I command you, come out of him, and enter him no more!'" (v. 25, *NKJV*).

Just as Jesus addressed this demon by its function, "deaf and dumb," so we assign the name "spirit of rejection" on the basis of how it manifests in our lives. When speaking about the spirit of rejection, we are referring to an assignment from hell—an evil spirit that attempts to exploit the pain, misfortune and mistakes that each of us might face in our lifelong pilgrimage. For example, though all of us can experience mood swings from time to time, this is not necessarily evidence of the presence of a spirit of rejection; but when there is a prolonged and persistent manifestation of rejection in our lives, it might be concluded that we have opened the door for this spirit to operate in us. That open door can take place when we agree with the evil spirit's lies or succumb to its temptations.

The first place in Scripture where the spirit of rejection is revealed is in the Garden of Eden, so we will take a view from the Garden to gather insights into the makeup and motive of rejection. Along the way, I hope to provide insights and answers to this most diabolical spirit. It is my firm belief that God has given us the authority through Jesus to deliver ourselves.

May God grant you freedom from the spirit of rejection!

Making It Personal

1. Consider a time in your life when everything changed because of a poor decision. How does the memory of that situation help you understand at least a little of what Adam and Eve felt after the Fall?

2. The Bible says that the Holy Spirit "will convict the world of sin, and of righteousness, and of judgment." At what times in your life has the Holy Spirit convicted you of sin, righteousness and/or judgment?

3. Can you think of any times when you or someone you know had an encounter with an evil spirit? Why do you think that was the case?

GETTING A FOOTHOLD

And do not give the devil a foothold.
EPHESIANS 4:27

How does the spirit of rejection get a foothold in our lives? How is it able to place us under bondage? Let's look at the two primary ways—through *trauma* and *generational iniquity*.

Trauma

Tim grew up in a loving, caring family, with attentive parents and brothers and sisters who all got along well with one another. Yet at the age of 35, he seemed to be suffering with the spirit of rejection and was acutely sensitive to how others treated him. If, for example, there was a social event in his church, he always expected to be left out or forgotten. He was almost paranoid, even believing at times that others conspired to keep him away. Nothing could have been further from the truth, of course. In fact, others were often puzzled by Tim's bizarre behavior and went out of their way to make sure he was invited or asked to serve. His pastor was also aware of the problem and spent considerable time discussing the situation with Tim.

Finally, as Tim began to share about his growing-up years, he recalled an incident that took place when he was five. After he was put to bed one evening, his parents, who were very active in their local church, went next door to talk with the neighbors about an upcoming church event. But they had no sooner stepped outside than Tim awoke and called for his mother. When she did not answer, he raced downstairs, searching for her, only to discover that his father was also missing. Scared and feeling abandoned, he began to cry. By the time his parents returned home about 10 minutes later, he was nearly hysterical. Not realizing the seriousness of Tim's emotional state, his parents made light of the matter and attempted to comfort him with milk and cookies. As far as they were concerned, the problem had been resolved.

Tim never forgot that frightening event. When Tim's pastor asked him to reflect on this incident, Tim realized that from that point on he remembered feeling that he would be abandoned again at any time. The wise pastor was then able to lead Tim through a prayer to break the power of the spirit of rejection over his life (later in this book I will share how you also can be set free from the spirit of rejection).

Of course, there are many forms of trauma equal to or more devastating than Tim's experience, such as divorce, abuse in all its forms, sudden death of a loved one, betrayal, abandonment and so on. But try telling that to five-year-old Tim. For him, it was devastatingly real and had an impact on his life all the way into adulthood.

We carry many such fears into our Christian walk, and many of us never quite get over them. We think that we just have to live with this overwhelming sense of rejection—that it's our lot in life. What we need to understand, however, is that what may seem burdensome to us may not be burdensome to others, and vice versa. Often, our strength is another person's weakness, and his or her strength is our weakness.

But to all, Jesus says, "[I have come] to heal the brokenhearted" (Luke 4:18, *NKJV*). It is not enough to say to someone, "Get over it! You're a Christian; all things have become new. Now deal with it!" Instead the Bible says we are to "carry each other's burdens, and in this way you will fulfill the law of Christ" (Gal. 6:2). Scripture also says, "For each one should carry his own load" (Gal. 6:5). On one hand, we are to help lift the burdens of others as we fulfill the law of Christ (which is to love one another, even as Christ loves us). On the other hand, we all must carry our own load, or bear a sense of personal responsibility. The point is that we are to lovingly help our brothers and sisters as they endure and ultimately overcome. After Cain killed Abel, God confronted Cain about it, and Cain countered with, "Am I my brother's keeper?" (Gen. 4:9). That question has echoed down through the ages. Are we our brother's keeper? Yes, in a sense we are. But it takes cooperation. Those who want help must also want freedom.

The good news is that God wants us free from the spirit of rejection even more than we do. In fact, freeing us is precisely why Jesus came—more about that later!

Generational Iniquity

The spirit of rejection can also gain a foothold through generational iniquity. To understand this, we need to clearly understand the word "iniquity." We often see this word used in the Old Testament. Here are a few examples:

- You shall not bow down to them nor serve them. For I, the LORD your God, am a jealous God, visiting the iniquity of the fathers on the children to the third and fourth generations of those who hate Me (Exod. 20:5, *NKJV*).

- Keeping mercy for thousands, forgiving iniquity and transgression and sin, by no means clearing the guilty, visiting the iniquity of the fathers upon the children and the children's children to the third and the fourth generation (Exod. 34:7, *NKJV*).

- All we like sheep have gone astray; we have turned, every one, to his own way; and the LORD has laid on Him the iniquity of us all (Isa. 53:6, *NKJV*).

- For I see that you are poisoned by bitterness and bound by iniquity (Acts 8:23, *NKJV*).

Iniquity Defined

Our nature apart from Christ is bent on living a life of lawlessness, or sin. Iniquity is a predisposition toward a particular sin. It is a perverseness and bent in our lives that leads us to commit the same sin over and over again. Often it's not just our sin—often such sins "run in the family." Our ancestors sinned, so we sin. We are all affected by the unrepented sin committed by previous generations.

Since iniquity is sin unconfessed, it is therefore excused, justified, denied and hidden; most of the time it is hidden from our own eyes. I would like to provide you with a definition of iniquity that comes close to the understanding of Scripture:

> Iniquity is gross injustice against God. When we cover our sin with excuses, rationalization, or justification, or say God is wrong in any judgment concerning that sin, it becomes iniquity. Therefore, iniquity is unrepented sin that becomes imbedded in our character, the spirit of which presses in on subsequent generations to the end that they might also be ensnared.

If, for example, a previous generation failed to repent of a predisposition toward abuse, then the spirit working behind that sin will press in on the next generation to bring abuse into the family. Does that mean that I am guilty of the sin of the previous generation? No. The Word of God makes that clear:

> Yet you ask, "Why does the son not share the guilt of his father?" since the son has done what is just and right and has been careful to keep all my decrees, he will surely live. The soul who sins is the one who will die. The son will not share the guilt of the father, nor will the father share the guilt of the son. The righteousness of the righteous man will be credited to him, and the wickedness of the wicked will be charged against him (Ezek. 18:19-20).

You and I will not be held accountable for the sins of any previous generation. However, if our forbears failed to repent of that iniquity, then the familiar spirits at work against that generation will press in on the following generation to cause them to perpetuate the iniquity. Thus it becomes generational iniquity.

If your mother or father was full of rejection and failed to deal with it, then there is a strong likelihood that the spirit of rejection will try to find its home in you. You are more vulnerable to that spirit than someone who grew up in a loving and wholesome environment of love and acceptance. However, the iniquity is only carried on if we submit to it and sin, and, in turn, become a person full of rejection who then rejects others.

Iniquity Broken

But how are we to find freedom from such iniquity? We certainly need to. Most of us suffering from addictive behavior will not receive our freedom until we deal with generational iniquity, which, in turn, leads us to wonder how we can get free if we are not aware of the sins in our family line. Many people cannot even recall the names of their great-grandparents, so how can they possibly be aware of what sins they committed? The point is that it is not necessary to know the details of their sins. What is important is to know that as believers in Jesus Christ we have the authority in His name to break every curse, vow and covenant that has ever been established in preceding generations.

> But He was wounded for our transgressions, He was bruised for our iniquities; the chastisement for our peace was upon Him, and by His stripes we are healed. All we like sheep have gone astray; we have turned, every one, to his own way; and the LORD has laid on Him the iniquity of us all (Isa. 53:5-6, *NKJV*).

Through His death on the cross, Jesus has borne all our sins and iniquities. Because of the death of Jesus on the cross, we can be set free from the consequences of the sins and iniquities of our ancestors. You can pray to break all generational iniquity that is attempting to assail your life.

Is it that simple? After all, the solution (God coming in the flesh to redeem us) was overwhelmingly difficult—and costly. This plan was established before the foundation of the earth, predetermined by the Godhead (Father, Son and Holy Spirit). The Father would send His Son to die upon the cross for our sins and iniquities, and then be raised by the Holy Spirit to sit at the right hand of the Father in all power and authority, which He has, by grace, also granted to His Bride, the Church. We now simply access that authority.

You might wonder why, if this is indeed true, more people aren't experiencing this freedom. The answer is sad but true: Believers are not aware of the need to break ties to ancestral iniquity.

Therefore my people are gone into captivity, because they have no knowledge (Isa. 5:13, *KJV*).

Perhaps this was true of you, too, before you began reading this book. But I encourage you now to grab hold of the truth in Jesus' name—and claim your freedom from the sins of your ancestors.

Biblical Examples of Iniquity

Generational iniquity is as old as humankind. And certainly God's chosen people were not immune from its effects. Their story can teach us a great deal about how one person's unrepented sin can bring devastation to the generations that follow.

David—Source of Sexual Iniquity

We're probably all familiar with the story of David and Bathsheba—how David caught sight of her as she was bathing on her roof. Once he decided to keep looking, he found himself starting down a dark road.

> The woman was very beautiful, and David sent someone to find out about her. The man said, "Isn't this Bathsheba, the daughter of Eliam and the wife of Uriah the Hittite?" Then David sent messengers to get her. She came to him, and he slept with her. (She had purified herself from her uncleanness.) Then she went back home (2 Sam. 11:2-4).

David was the tenth generation from the line of Judah, who had sex with Tamar, his daughter-in-law (see Gen. 38:1-26). David's son Amnon continued the same abuse in raping his half-sister (see 2 Sam. 13:1-22). David's son Absalom slept with David's concubines in the sight of all Israel (see 2 Sam. 16:22). Iniquity was at work, causing division, disruption and destruction.

Abraham—Source of Iniquity of Marital Abuse

Then we come to Abram (Abraham), who out of fear, pretended that his wife, Sarai (Sarah), was not his wife but his sister. The first time Abraham employed this deception was when he and his household went down to Egypt.

> As he was about to enter Egypt, he said to his wife Sarai, "I know what a beautiful woman you are. When the Egyptians see you, they will say, 'This is his wife.' Then

they will kill me but will let you live. Say you are my sister, so that I will be treated well for your sake and my life will be spared because of you" (Gen. 12:11-13).

And the rest of the story isn't surprising: The Pharaoh did indeed notice Sarah's beauty. So she was brought to live in the palace as his wife. Of course, as Abraham had predicted, he himself was treated very well. But God wasn't pleased with the arrangement, so He inflicted suffering upon the Pharaoh, who soon realized what he had done.

> So Pharaoh summoned Abram. "What have you done to me?" he said. "Why didn't you tell me she was your wife? Why did you say, 'She is my sister,' so that I took her to be my wife? Now then, here is your wife. Take her and go!" Then Pharaoh gave orders about Abram to his men, and they sent him on his way, with his wife and everything he had (Gen. 12:18-20).

One would think, of course, that Abraham had learned his lesson. But the iniquity continued. When Abraham and Sarah moved on to Gerar, he told the king Abimelech that Sarah was his sister. And so he took her into his household.
Once again, God intervened to prevent further abuse.

> But God came to Abimelech in a dream one night and said to him, "You are as good as dead because of the woman you have taken; she is a married woman."
> Now Abimelech had not gone near her, so he said, "Lord, will you destroy an innocent nation? Did he not

say to me, 'She is my sister,' . . . I have done this with a clear conscience and clean hands" (Gen. 20:3-5).

Then Abimelech returned Sarah to Abraham, telling them that they could live anywhere they wished in his land. And it seems that Abraham got the message at last.

Yet this is not the end of this particular story. This very same sin appears again in his family—only this time it is his son, Isaac, who, out of fear, puts his wife at risk to save his own life. "When the men of that place asked him about his wife, he said, 'She is my sister,' because he was afraid to say, 'She is my wife.' He thought, 'The men [the Philistines] of this place might kill me on account of Rebekah, because she is beautiful'" (Gen. 26:7).

Soon after it was discovered that Isaac had lied—that Rebekah was his wife, not his sister. When questioned why he had deceived the Philistines, Isaac admitted that he had feared for his life. Then the king of the Philistines rebuked him: "What is this you have done to us? One of the men might well have slept with your wife, and you would have brought guilt upon us" (Gen. 26:10).

Perhaps now that you know what generational iniquity looks like, you're no longer reflecting on these Bible stories. Perhaps you've come to realize that such iniquity might well exist in your own family. If so, that's a good first step.

Recognizing and Breaking the Bondage

From here, if you truly seek freedom for yourself, you need to identify the tell-tale signs of generational iniquity. Examine your own family, past and present. See if any of the following effects caused by the spirit of rejection are evidenced in the lives of your loved ones.

- Fathers failing to show love and affection to their daughters, prompting them to search for comfort and approval from other men

- Fathers failing to validate their sons, causing them to look for approval but rarely finding it from others, growing up insecure and failure-prone

- Mothers failing to nurture their families, leaving a great void that is passed on to future generations

- Sexual abuse within the family, creating shattered lives incapable of maintaining healthy relationships

- Loss of identity due to comparing and competing siblings

- Parents robbing their children of quality time, thereby robbing them of personal value

The list could cover 10 pages. The tragedy is that in most all these types of situations, the parents have themselves been victims of the same kind of neglect or sinful behavior, and by not repenting, they have perpetuated the behavior to the next generation. We are not just discussing theological issues here; we are dealing with pain and torment on a global scale. This stain of generational iniquity has become part of the fabric of millions of homes around the world.

As president of Cleansing Stream Ministries, I have traveled extensively with my wife, Karen. We have seen firsthand how, in this country as well as in other nations, generational iniquity has taken its toll. This root of rejection can be pulled up and cast out, but we must first see generational iniquity repented of, renounced and broken.

I now offer this prayer as something you can proclaim by faith in Jesus Christ.

Prayer of Freedom from Generational Sin and Iniquity

I thank You, Lord, for setting me free from darkness and establishing me in the kingdom of Light. I accept what Jesus has done on the cross for me, taking away all my sin and shame, and bearing my iniquity upon Himself. I am now a new creation and a member of Your heavenly family. I proclaim Jesus as my Lord and Savior.

As a member of the human family, I confess that my previous generations and I have been lawless and have broken Your commandments. I particularly confess involvement in _____ *[name the specific involvement]. I forgive and release all previous generations for how their sin has affected me. I also confess and repent of any way in which I have personally been involved with this sin, and I ask that You forgive me.*

In Jesus' name, I confess and renounce every covenant, curse and agreement made by my ancestors or me with this sin and others, known and unknown. I revoke and cancel every covenant or blood covenant that in any way opened the door of demonic activity against me or my family. I revoke any and all agreements with the purposes of Satan and the powers of darkness. I choose to be in agreement with God's purposes and align myself with His will. I thank You that through the precious blood of Jesus, I am cleansed from all sin. I take the Sword of the Spirit and by faith cut away every entanglement, every cord and all generational iniquity in the name of Jesus Christ, by the power of His blood.

I thank You, Lord, for bearing all my iniquity, and I now claim freedom from all curses, covenants and agreements—all hereditary diseases and other consequences from previous generations. In the name of Jesus, amen!

Possessing Your Possession

Perhaps generational sin has been preventing you from walking in the inheritance God has in store for you. Now that you have repented, you may well be wondering what God is waiting for. After all, there is nothing separating you from His will—every barrier has been removed. So what's the holdup?

The answer lies in Scripture: When the children of Israel, led by Moses and subsequently by Joshua, came to the Promised Land, there was great hope and expectation of quickly and easily taking possession of it. It was promised to Abraham; all of it was theirs by right, given to them by God. But what they didn't understand was that it was going to take time. They had to dispossess their enemies before they could possess the land for themselves. There would be warfare and casualties, trials and temptations along the way. There would be times of correction from God and times of untold blessings. But it would not be done overnight. They would possess their possession little by little:

> I will not drive them out in a single year, because the land would become desolate and the wild animals too numerous for you. Little by little I will drive them out from before you, until you have increased enough to take possession of the land (Exod. 23:29-30).

We, also, through the process of sanctification and spiritual warfare, learn how to take full possession of all the rich promises in Christ Jesus. They are ours by right. They have been granted to us through the cross of Jesus Christ. His blood has paid for it all. In the words of our Savior, "It is finished!"

> Who *delivered* us from so great a death, and *does deliver* us; in whom we trust that He *will still deliver* us (2 Cor. 1:10, *NKJV*, emphasis added).

And so you and I will take possession, little by little, of all that God has purposed for us.

> Now we see but a poor reflection as in a mirror; then we shall see face to face. Now I know in part; then I shall know fully, even as I am fully known (1 Cor. 13:12).

Making It Personal

1. Can you think of a traumatic event in your own life that might have given a foothold to the spirit of rejection? How does the memory of that event affect the way you felt as you read Tim's story?

2. Are there any problems in your family that you think might actually be "inherited" generational iniquities? How does that possibility change the way you view these problems?

3. How does the knowledge that God told Israel they would take possession of the Promised Land "little by little" help you?

GOD WANTS YOU FREE!

And now these three remain: faith, hope, and love.
But the greatest of these is love.

1 CORINTHIANS 13:13

Dictionaries vary in their definitions of the word "rejection." In one, I found this statement: Rejection is the act of being rejected. Wow! Isn't that enlightening?! A more helpful definition of rejection is simply "the absence of love." I don't think it could be more clearly stated. Rejection is the act of denying love to someone.

Why would God be so interested in dealing with this evil spirit of rejection? I believe it is because of Jesus' experience of rejection on Earth, and especially His rejection on the cross. Rejection goes to the very heart of God Himself.

Sammy might have been only nine years old, but he understood the heart of God better than most adults. Sammy attended a private Christian school. His parents had divorced when he was six, but Sammy's father continued to provide for his son financially, even though he had moved thousands of miles away to start a new life with a woman he had met online. Sammy wanted for nothing materially, and his mother did her best to try to fulfill her son's emotional and spiritual needs—and she never missed any of Sammy's school functions. So when the kinder-garten through sixth grade students performed an Easter play for their families, Sammy's mother sat right up front where she knew her son could see her.

When the reenactment of the crucifixion had ended, climaxing with Jesus' triumphant resurrection and ascension into heaven, one of the teachers took the microphone and asked the children what they thought was the most painful thing Jesus had experi-enced in His torturous death. One child said it was when the spikes were driven through His hands and feet. Another said it was when the soldiers whipped Him, while yet another thought it was when they pressed the crown of thorns onto His head.

And then Sammy raised his hand. His mother was surprised, because her son was shy and seldom spoke out in a crowd. She also knew this portion of the program was unrehearsed, so she won-dered what Sammy's answer would be. When she heard it, her heart was crushed.

"I think it was when His Father turned away from Him," Sammy said.

A hush fell over the auditorium as the impact of that little nine-year-old boy's statement found its mark. From the youngest to the oldest, all seemed mesmerized at the realization of the depth of rejection Jesus had experienced as He hung on the cross, the weight of the sins of the world upon Him, and cried out, "My God, My God, why have you forsaken me?" (Matt. 27:46).

If anyone knows about rejection, it is God.

- Lucifer warred against God, rejecting His authority, and so was cast down to the earth.

- Adam and Eve rejected His Word and His ways, bringing about the fall of humankind.
- God sent His prophets to the people, but the people killed them and rejected His love.
- Jesus was rejected by those He came to save.
- Jesus' disciples rejected Him in His hour of greatest need.
- Christ became sin for us on the cross; darkness fell, and He was left completely alone.
- Throughout history much of the world has rejected—and continues to reject—the love and sacrifice God has provided to bring them to salvation.
- Many believers today compromise and reject God's Word.

God's Plan: Love

Throughout recorded history, the spirit of rejection has been front and center. But we have hope, because, through His gracious providence, God's plan of redemption and reconciliation calls for the eradication of rejection. If there is one ministry that each of us has, regardless of our individual gifting, it is this:

> Now all things are of God, who has reconciled us to Himself through Jesus Christ, and has given us the ministry of reconciliation, that is, that God was in Christ reconciling the world to Himself, not imputing their trespasses to them, and has committed to us the word of reconciliation (2 Cor. 5:18-19, *NKJV*).

The heart of God is reconciliation—which necessarily means the end of rejection. We can see God's motivation in dealing with the spirit of rejection in one very small verse in the New Testament:

> For when we place our faith in Christ Jesus, it makes no difference to God whether we are circumcised or not circumcised. What is important is *faith expressing itself in love* (Gal. 5:6, *NLT*, emphasis added).

Please take note of the last sentence. Other Bible translations read, "faith, working through love." These four words are packed with meaning.

If you are going to have faith in your life—God's kind of faith—then it has to be expressed through love. If you are weak in faith, it means that your love is also weak. No love, no faith. Weak love, weak faith. Strong love, strong faith.

Satan's Counterstrategy

It is here—in the realm of love—where we can begin to see why the devil has done everything in his power to establish the spirit of rejection in the human race and why he has sought to bring such a rift between God and humankind. He continues to wreak havoc among us in order to deplete the human race of love. I do not believe the devil has the power to create every destructive scenario we ever experience. However, I am convinced that he will do everything he can to take advantage of every human tragedy and, in the process, shatter love. Why? Because he is innately heinous? Yes, but that is not the whole of it.

The enemy of our souls is well aware of the truth that faith works through love. He also knows that most of us would not surrender our faith in Jesus Christ. So how does He weaken our faith? Quite simply, he seeks to deplete us of all love. In so doing, our faith is weakened and we become paralyzed, unable to advance the kingdom of God. No love, no faith—because faith works through love.

Speaking of Satan, Jesus said, "The thief does not come except to steal and kill and destroy" (John 10:10). The word "steal" in this verse is quite interesting. In the original language it is the word *klepto*, from which we get the word "kleptomaniac." A kleptomaniac is a thief—a particular kind of thief. If you were to inadvertently invite a kleptomaniac into your house, he might pose as a friend or deliveryman. He would steal from you, but not at gunpoint. He would wait until your back was turned, then take something valuable and slip it into his pocket. You might smile and shake his hand as he left, never knowing that a valuable was now missing. If he came into your home a few more times, you might come to the conclusion that every time he came, you ended up with something missing. It would not take long before all the valuable things in your house were gone.

That is the way Satan works. He comes to you by stealth—under the radar. How does this work out in practical ways? Let me give you an example.

Bob and Mary were Christians who had begun to fall on hard times. When Bob lost his job, Mary was a stay-in-the-home mom, helping to rear the children. Bob became frustrated when he could not find work. He began to get upset with Mary, saying that she was not doing enough to help out. He began to put pressure on her to work outside the home. Mary felt that the children were at risk if she did. She began to accuse Bob of being lazy and not trying hard enough to find a new job. Words of blame began to fly, and Bob and Mary placed each other under condemnation.

Love was at an all-time low in their marriage. They stopped going to church. At one time they had prayed together, but no longer. Before their troubles came, they had shared their faith with others, but that endeavor had also come to an end. Their marriage was in serious trouble, and they were no longer effectively advancing the gospel.

Satan probably had not caused Bob to lose his job. But once it happened, the devil worked tirelessly to bring rejection into Bob and Mary's home. He tempted them to speak words to cut and wound each other, and they were falling for the ploy. Satan was introducing the spirit of rejection in order to deplete their love and weaken their faith. Little by little, he began to pilfer the valuables from their home.

What was he stealing? Look at Galatians for a list of the things he steals.

> But the fruit of the Spirit is love, joy, peace, longsuffering, kindness, goodness, faithfulness, gentleness and self-control. Against such things there is no law (Gal. 5:22-23).

The very fruit of the Spirit—love, joy, peace, longsuffering, kindness, goodness, faithfulness, gentleness, self-control—is exactly what the enemy of our souls comes to steal from us.

Abundant Life

In John 10:10, Jesus revealed to us that the enemy wants to rip us off, to steal everything of value from our lives. Aren't you glad there is a second half to that verse? Jesus said the enemy had his ways, but Jesus had something to declare in the midst of it: "I have come that they may have life, and that they may have it more abundantly" (John 10:10, *NKJV*).

Jesus has come that we might have life more abundantly. That means that whereas the enemy wants to take from us all that is precious and good in life, Jesus wants to add to our life quality and goodness. He wants all the fruit of the Spirit to have full expression in our attitudes and actions. Instead of depleting us of love, He desires to fill us with the love of God. And He will do everything in His power to make known to us that we are fully accepted, that He will never leave or forsake us (see Heb. 13:5).

With this in mind, let us step into the Garden and observe the walls that were built there—walls of rejection behind which the spirit of rejection works. We'll see how they get established and how they can be broken down. We will also see the overwhelming love of God at work.

So, in the next chapters, let us take another view from the Garden.

Making It Personal

1. Rejection is the act of denying love to someone. When you read that statement, particularly in light of Sammy's story, what emotions are stirred inside of you?

2. Now consider this statement: The heart of God is reconciliation. How do your emotions change when you consider the truth and possibilities of that statement?

3. Have you ever felt as if there was a thief in your home, stealing your joy and your peace—everything that was good and right? Understanding that God wants to restore those good things that were stolen from you, what might you do to cooperate with God to see that happen?

PART THREE

WALLS IN THE GARDEN

CHAPTER 7

THE REJECTION OF GOD

So when the woman saw that the tree was good for food and pleasing to the
eye, also desirable for gaining wisdom, she took some [of its fruit] and ate it.
She also gave some to her husband, who was with her, and he ate it.

GENESIS 3:6

Nothing impacts the human heart more than rejection. When we open the door to this spirit, rejection begins to encase our heart. It stunts our growth in Christ and impacts every relationship. We allow walls to be built, thinking they keep bad things out. But they also keep good things locked up inside.

The walls of rejection that we'll focus on are the walls that keep you from being all that God intends for you. To knock down these walls might feel a little threatening or scary because we get comfortable with our limitations, and change can be threatening. But allowing the walls to remain will keep us from God's best for our lives.

In John 5, the story is told of Jesus coming to the Pool of Bethesda. As He walked in, He approached a very sick man: "When Jesus saw him lying there, and knew that he already had been in that condition a long time, He said to him, 'Do you want to be made well?'" (v. 6, *NKJV*).

Notice the question: "Do you want to be made well?" What an odd thing to ask a sick person! The man had been in that condition for a long time, yet Jesus asked him if he wanted to be well. I believe the question could have been asked this way: "Do you want to change?" From the exchange that followed, it became evident that the man had long since given up the expectation of being made well and had become comfortable with his limitations.

We too can become comfortable within the walls of rejection because they seem to offer us safety. We adjust to them and become fearful of making changes; but when we break down the walls of rejection, our life becomes richer and fuller. In order for that to happen, we have to do some serious and honest soul-searching and have a willingness to confess and repent for wrong attitudes and actions.

Repent, Renounce and Break

When dealing with and breaking demonic strongholds, there are three steps that need to be taken: repent, renounce and break.

As Christians, most of us are acquainted with the term "repent," but few are aware of the need to renounce and break. Let's take a brief look at each step.

Repent

Let's look at the first word, "repent." Breaking this powerful little word apart, we see that it literally means "again (re) humble (penitent)." One who is penitent expresses humble, or regretful, sorrow for sins or offenses. "To repent" means to come back to that place of humility and sorrow over sin. We are coming back to the One who grants forgiveness. We are not trying something new or different; we are reaffirming our need for the Savior, Deliverer and Redeemer, Jesus. "Salvation is found in no one else, for there is no other name under heaven given to [humanity] by which we must be saved" (Acts 4:12).

If there is no repentance, then we continue to walk in darkness, deceived by the enemy. And if we continue to be deceived, we remain in bondage. "Therefore say to the house of Israel, 'This is what the Sovereign LORD says: Repent! Turn from your idols and renounce all your detestable practices!'" (Ezek. 14:6).

Renounce

"To renounce" means to give up, refuse, or resign by formal declaration. Whereas repenting is directed toward God, renouncing is directed toward the enemy. When we renounce, we are canceling any and all agreements we have made with the enemy (e.g., anything that contradicts God's Word). We are making a formal declaration that we no longer align ourselves with things that oppose God. You might think to yourself, *Well, I've never made an agreement with Satan.* Yet whenever we align ourselves with his evil purposes, we end up granting him authority to work in our lives: "Don't you know that when you offer yourselves to someone to obey him as slaves, you are slaves to the one whom you obey" (Rom. 6:16).

Our words are significant, but God has given us authority in Jesus' name to cancel any spiritually binding contract. Many believers repent of their sins before God, only to find themselves in a losing tug-of-war with the enemy, repeating their failures. We must shut the door on the devil, refusing by formal declaration to walk in the ways of the past. Renouncing is the means by which we cut off any legal right for Satan to bind or torment us. This is the way we resist him—the only way we can be free of him and his hold over our lives: "Submit yourselves, then to God [repent]. Resist the devil [renounce], and he will flee from you" (Jas. 4:7).

If our words are contrary to God's, then we have aligned ourselves with the works of darkness. To be free from the works of darkness, we must counter those words with God's Word, thus renouncing the hidden works of shame.

> But we have renounced the hidden things of shame, not walking in craftiness nor handling the word of God deceitfully, but by manifestation of the truth commending ourselves to every man's conscience in the sight of God (2 Cor. 4:2, *NKJV*).

> The night is far spent, the day is at hand. Therefore let us cast off the works of darkness, and let us put on the armor of light (Rom. 13:12, *NKJV*).

Break

Once we repent, we have the right to cancel or renounce any legal hold the enemy had over us; the yoke of bondage can be broken off our lives. God loves to see us come to the place where yokes are broken, and it thoroughly frustrates the enemy!

> "In that day," declares the LORD Almighty, "I will break the yoke off their necks and will tear off their bonds; no longer will foreigners enslave them. Instead, they will serve the LORD their God" (Jer. 30:8-9).

> In that day their burden will be lifted from your shoulders, their yoke from your neck; the yoke will be broken (Isa. 10:27).

The Four Walls

Take a look at the diagram at the beginning of this chapter of four square walls surrounding a heart and a crown. That heart could be your heart. The crown represents the lordship of Christ. You will see that as we break down each wall, the heart inside will grow, along with the crown of the Lord. As you and I become free from rejection, we have a greater capacity to love God and to love others. Remember, rejection is the absence of love. So get ready to be loved! And, in turn, you will be able to offer love.

Rejecting God

The first wall around your heart represents your rejection of God. This is the first wall to go up. If it never goes up, neither will the others. Once it does go up, however, everything else will follow. Most of us don't think of God as being rejected. We are far more concerned about our own sense of rejection:

- what we feel
- how we've been treated
- the injustice done to us
- fear of being hurt again
- taking our pain out on others

But before any of this takes place, we first reject God, though most of us stay blind to this fact. We will consider this idea with a view from the Garden of Eden. Let's go there and see how each of these walls goes up. We'll follow the lead of Scripture, as these four walls are described in several places in the Bible. Now you'll have an opportunity to see it in your own life.

In chapter 2, "The Great Seduction," I remarked on what appeared to be the process by which Eve was deceived. While it is impossible to know exactly the process of thinking that took place, we know enough to make certain conclusions:

- The amount of time between the first encounter with the serpent and the act of taking the fruit is not known. It may have taken place over a period of days, weeks or months.

- Eve had no previous experience with deception.

- She began to believe the lie that God was holding back something of value.

- It is likely that she no longer felt important to God.

- It is likely, because of the lies, that she was feeling rejected by God.

- The attraction of something forbidden, coupled with
  the sense of rejection, prompted her to act in disobedience.

- Pride and unbelief were birthed, which then opened the
  door to the spirit of rejection.

Whether we can correctly discern the process of thinking in either Eve or Adam is irrelevant to the fact that they broke the command, thrusting themselves and their lineage into a fallen state. Whatever the thought process, the point is that they reject-ed God. They rejected His word, His ways and His love. When they did so, they opened the door to the spirit of rejection.

Reaping the Consequences

The enemy waits on tiptoe for any opportunity to ensnare us. If we violate a command, we become a slave to the one we have obeyed. If we lie, we become subject to a lying spirit. If we are immoral, we become subject to an unclean spirit (see Rom. 6:16). So if we reject, we become subject to the spirit of rejection.

When Adam and Eve rejected God, they became lawbreak-ers. We also become lawbreakers when we disobey His Word. Here's a partial list of what begins to be established in our lives as a result:

- *Rebellion*—Since rebellion is the act of disobedience, a spirit of rebellion then becomes our companion, causing further rejection and alienation from God and others.

- *Self-Will*—Choosing to be independent from God, we cease to be led by the Spirit, instead embracing self-centeredness and self-motivation, adding fuel to the spirit of rejection as we care less for others and more for ourselves.

- *Unforgiveness*—We begin to blame God and others for their apparent failure toward us. Eve needed to repent for entrapping Adam, and Adam to repent for failing to effectively love and protect Eve. We often find ourselves in the same dilemma. Our rebellion leads to pain in those around us, requiring us to seek forgiveness.

- *Bitterness*—Since our actions often lead to great loss, we become bitter against God for those losses, even though they are of our own doing. This continues to feed the rejection in us, as it becomes deeply rooted and affects every area of our lives.

- *Resentment*—Resentment builds toward God for allowing bad things to happen, and toward others for not protecting or taking care of us as we think they should have. As a result, we begin to reject others, and they begin to reject us for our bad behavior.

- *Unbelief*—When we choose not to believe God's Word, we then become subject to the spirit of unbelief. From there it is not a long stretch until we become doubters and cynics.

- *Anger*—We become angry for not getting what we wanted and for not getting our own way. This spills out upon our children, causing them to blame themselves and opening up the door to the spirit of rejection in their lives.

- *Revenge*—Being overwhelmed by rejection, we begin to lash out at those around us, usually our family, and cause a further rift.

These are the consequences of rejecting God. Our freedom comes as we repent and renounce our sin of rejecting the very One who has always loved us and who is seeking our well-being. When we don't receive what we want, it is possible to believe that God is holding out on us, that He is being a cosmic killjoy and that for some perverse reason He likes to prevent us from having something in which we see no harm. But we fail to see the truth: "and to observe the LORD'S commands and decrees that I am giving you today *for your own good*" (Deut. 10:13, emphasis added).

God is our Creator. He knows us perfectly. He knows the heartache and misery we will face when we reject His commands, for they were given to us for our good. How many of us have made decisions in the full knowledge that we were going against His Word? Can we recall the consequences? Can we remember the pain we had to endure for not listening to His warnings? We must first break down this wall of rejecting God, and then we will be free to bring down the other walls.

Examining Our Hearts

Take the time to seek the Lord and ask Him to reveal to your mind the times when you have rejected His Word, His ways or His love. Once these things have been made known to you, read the prayer at the end of this chapter out loud, making it a personal declaration of faith.

I cannot emphasize enough the importance of our coming to grips with pride as we approach this subject. Pride will keep us from seeing the truth and acknowledging God's rule in our lives as it blinds us and makes us defensive. Unmasking pride can be the most painful experience in life—but it can also be the most beneficial.

I recall when I was an associate pastor and administrator at a large church in Texas. My background before accepting that position was as an executive with a major Christian publishing house. I had developed a certain worldly mentality and was driven to get things done. My management skills had definitely not been sanctified. There were times when the way I conducted myself was not Spirit-led. Too often I leveraged people to accomplish my objectives. As a result, several good people felt manipulated by me.

Of course, I was blind to it all. Pride is very subtle and can be rationalized away. There came a time, however, when the Lord had to deal with pride in my life because He was preparing me to be a pastor after His own heart. Soon a situation arose in the church that resulted in many accusations flying around. The senior pastor had fallen into immorality, and there came an intense pressure against all pastoral staff. Many people in the church felt terribly wounded and betrayed. It was a most unhappy season in our lives. The Lord told me to be quiet and not defend myself. "Chris," He said, "you can defend yourself, or you can be quiet and allow Me to be your defense. What do you want?"

I said, "You're my defense, Lord." So I kept my mouth shut during this heavy period of accusations. At times, I wanted to run and hide. At other times, I wanted to defend myself and retaliate. It all came to a head one evening as I was pouring my heart out to God. The Holy Spirit opened my eyes to see that at times, I *had been controlling and manipulative*, walking over the feelings of others to get my own way. I was devastated. I suddenly realized that some of the criticism was valid. Among the onslaught of words was an element of truth, and that hurt.

Then the Lord said to me, "I want you to make a list of the people I will show you that you have offended. You are to go to them and confess your sin of pride and ask for their forgiveness."

I said, "But, Lord, they have said and done some wrong things as well. They've spoken behind my back and said many untruths. How do I handle that?"

He said, "You take care of your end of things and I will take care of the rest."

And so I made my list, and then one by one made appointments to meet with each person on my list. Some were at first suspicious of my intentions, but I determined that I would not bring up any faults other than my own. Many of those private meetings ended up with all of us crying and confessing our faults one to the other. To this day, if I were to come back to that town, the very people I met with to ask for their forgiveness would be the first to warmly greet me. God did an amazing thing as a result of that situation, but not before I came to grips with the sin of pride in my life.

To my readers, I ask that you please invite the Holy Spirit to search your heart and see where pride might be lurking. Job 41 speaks entirely about pride. Leviathan is the name given to this spirit. I encourage you to stop and read Job 41. The last verse reads, "He looks down on all that are haughty; he is king over all that are proud" (v. 34).

Pride was found in Lucifer; as a result, he was cast out of heaven, bringing down a third of the angels with him. We must humble ourselves before God, or pride will take us down as well.

Search me, O God, and know my heart; test me and know my anxious thoughts. See if there is any offensive way in me, and lead me in the way everlasting (Ps. 139:23-24).

Prayer of Repentance for Rejecting God

Father God, I'm sorry for all the times and all the ways I have rejected You. Please forgive me. I repent for not believing You, for not listening to You and for refusing Your love. I repent for not trusting You, and for doubting Your love for me. I repent for all the stubbornness, pride, self-will and rebellion that either I or my family have walked in.

In the name of Jesus, I renounce all rejection of God. I renounce all involvement with any spirit that would lead me to reject God. I renounce and break all vows and covenants, all soul ties and generational ties that would bind me to the rejection of God. I choose to love God with all my heart, with all my soul and with all my mind. I renounce every spirit that has to do with the rejection of God. And now, as a choice of my will, I break down this wall—in the mighty name of Jesus, amen.

Making It Personal

1. What was your first reaction when you saw the diagram of the boxes at the beginning of this chapter? How did you react after reading the chapter and then revisiting the diagram?

2. In your own words, define the words "repent," "renounce" and "break."

3. In what areas of your life have you put up walls and refused to let God come in? How do you think those areas might change if you knocked down the walls and invited Him inside?

SELF-REJECTION

And the eyes of them both were opened, and they knew that they were naked;
and they sewed fig leaves together, and made themselves aprons.

GENESIS 3:7, *KJV*

I have only tinkered around in the garden from time to time—though I am no horticulturist—but I think I can safely say that fig leaves will eventually turn brown. It would not take long for them to wither and die once cut away from their source. So why would Adam and Eve choose to wear fig leaves? Didn't they know the leaves were temporal? Didn't they know that in a short time they would have to be replaced? Yet aren't we the same? Don't we react similarly when confronted with shame?

It doesn't have to be that way. When confronted with shame, we have a choice. One choice is to allow the Lord to deal with shame as He does with all sin. The other is to try to cover ourselves up with something of our own making. This chapter deals with the wrong responses we make to the emotion of shame.

The root of self-rejection and self-hatred is shame, but often that shame is false. I speak with hundreds of people every year who have been abused and molested. Almost without question, they feel a sense of shame, as if they were in some way responsible. Not all shame is a result of personal sin. Yet during our Cleansing Stream retreats we minister to those who have been abused, and part of that ministry requires repentance.

You might ask, "If they were not responsible for the abuse they received, then why should they repent?" That is a good question. The answer is that they don't have to repent over the act of abuse, but most people usually need to repent over their responses to that abuse. As I said before, because of our different personalities, we all respond differently to the tragedies in our lives. In some the response is perfectionism; in others the response may be anger and unforgiveness. In still others the response may be some form of self-mutilation. It is often our responses for which we must repent. Whether our reaction is to do harm to others by what we say or how we treat them, or to do harm to ourselves, either response requires repentance to God for unbelief or pride leading to self-rejection.

Cover-Ups

When shame hits us, our first reaction is to cover up. It is interesting how the expression "cover-up" has found its way into our vocabulary. In news journalism, reporters want to "cover" a story—they want to examine every facet of an event, dig into the history of the people being focused on, and find out everything they can in order to write an accurate (it is hoped) and interesting story. Yet often these reporters find much less than the whole truth—they have a keen sense of when the truth is being masked by a "cover-up." When they smell a cover-up, they go after it like a dog after a flea.

When a cover-up is taking place, the truth is being hidden. The cover-up can play out in a number of different ways.

- *Denial.* An attempt to downplay or deny the truth. In some cases it might be stated outright: "No, I did not do that!" or "You must have mistaken me for someone else!" But with most of us, denial takes on far more subtle characteristics. If the pain of rejection is so severe, we often turn to someone or something other than God for comfort, as happened in Ron's case. Ron had been rejected by his dad when he was a little boy, though he actively sought his dad's approval throughout his lifetime. One year after college, Ron's dad promised him he would inherit the family business. Years passed and nothing more was said about the promise. Ron became increasingly angry and turned to alcohol and gambling. Now, his dad was both an alcoholic and a gambler, so Ron needed to be healed of the place of iniquity passed on from his dad. Little did Ron know that his dad's dad was an alcoholic living on skid row—and he had rejected *his* son when he was young. The spirit of addiction was passed on from one generation to the next because the iniquity had never been healed.

- *Misdirection.* Like a fox doubling back on its track, people who use this tactic attempt to divert those seeking the truth by giving them false leads—encouraging them to focus anywhere but on the real truth. They are experts at changing the subject when the spotlight focuses on them and their actions. Though they may succeed in getting the focus off themselves and onto someone else, they have done nothing to free themselves of the shame that continues to plague their lives.

- *Character alteration.* A recently convicted mass murderer was discovered to be a Boy Scout leader and an active member of his church. He was not skulking about in the daytime; he was feigning who he was to everyone around him, including his family, when in reality he was quite the opposite. You don't have to be a mass murderer to lead a double life—this tactic can be used by anyone who has a sin to hide.

- *Isolation.* If you want to avoid confrontation, then hide away so that no one will notice you. This was Adam and Eve's response, and it is a common response among those who want to cover up their shame rather than deal with it God's way. As Adam and Eve discovered, it is impossible to hide from God. He already knows where we are and what we've done, and He stands ready

to forgive us and set us free if we will just come out of
hiding and submit to Him.

There may be other ways of trying to cover up, but you get
the point. Each of us behaves in a slightly different manner,
depending on our personality and experience. Shame is such a
powerful emotion that it can cause an otherwise intelligent person to behave in a quite bizarre manner.

The spirit of self-rejection (sometimes called self-hatred) is
one of the most vicious. It is very easy to assess people from
their outward behavior. Redemption, however, calls for us to
examine what is behind the behavior. In the following pages, I
will share with you some observations of those who have been
plagued with a spirit of self-rejection.

False Shame

Rejection and shame both have deception at their root. It is
quite possible to feel what we call "false shame." Much shame
stems from actions on our part or on the part of others that is
directly related to personal failure—the kind of failure that
would be a violation of God's moral law. There is a shame, however, that comes from a totally deceptive source, as in the case
of Alastair Roy. Here is his story—in his own words.

One of the areas where God recently healed me was in
the area of "false guilt." The Holy Spirit will bring us to
repentance through guilty feelings, but false guilt is
not from God. False guilt is from the one known as the

"accuser," the very one who first drew Adam and Eve into sin and its resulting guilt and shame. In their case, of course, their guilt and shame were real results of their own wrong choices. False guilt is different, but it is very subtle and can deceive us into thinking it is our guilt. Satan can take circumstances that occur in our lives and exploit them for his purposes. He did just that in my own life, resulting in making me feel responsible for something that was not my responsibility—until God intervened.

It began when I was 20 months old, when I was seriously scalded when I accidentally pulled a kettle of boiling water down on myself. My injuries were so serious I almost died. I spent 4 months in the hospital, and I still bear the scars 55 years later. My father blamed my mother for leaving me exposed to that danger. In all my lifetime I never knew him to love her, care for her, sleep with her or respect her. When I was 18 years old, I left home to join the police force (Royal Ulster Constabulary); soon after, my parents parted and eventually divorced. A few years ago my wife, Pauline, and I were at a ministry training conference in England, and I began speaking with another person who was taking the [Cleansing Stream] course. I related what I've just shared here, and the Lord seemed to show me through this man that I had taken responsibility for the breakup of my parents' marriage.

Now, rationally, I knew it wasn't my fault, but somehow in my soul I had taken on a perception in my life that it was. But the truth was that Mum had left the fire guard off and nipped out to get coal for two minutes. I then had pulled the kettle over myself, and Dad blamed her. It wasn't her fault, and it certainly wasn't mine, as I was less than two years old. But because I knew that incident had spurred my father's rejection of my mother, over the years I had embraced false guilt for their resulting divorce. Satan is clever; he knows about deception and bondage, and throughout my life, he used every possible opportunity to reinforce my false guilt.

In 1971, I was a young 22-year-old police sergeant on the border with the Irish Republic. It was in the early years of that vicious 30-year terrorist campaign in Northern Ireland, and one morning I detailed a young constable under my command for duty at a security checkpoint in the town of Newry. I told him to wear his bulletproof jacket, but they were cumbersome things in those days, and he didn't want to wear it. Because it wasn't compulsory, I didn't insist. A couple of hours later Davy was shot in the back while trying to prevent a terrorist bomb attack—and he died in my arms. He was only 19 years old, and his wife had their first child a week later. If he'd been wearing his flak jacket he may have lived, though we can't know that for sure. His death was not my fault, and yet I felt responsible. False guilt and shame were reinforced.

Then, a couple of years later, Pauline and I wanted to go to a dance in a nearby town, so I asked my friend Sergeant Jimmy Hunter to swap duties with me so we'd be free to go. While we were gone, I.R.A. terrorist gunmen ambushed Jimmy's patrol car, and Jimmy was shot dead in the front passenger seat of that vehicle where I should have been sitting. I didn't know about it until the next day, and even then I wouldn't believe it. I drove to the hospital where they had taken him, and then watched as they pulled out the freezer tray in the morgue. There was Jimmy, lying there in full uniform. It wasn't my fault, but false guilt was reinforced yet again.

Today the Holy Spirit may be saying to you, "It is not your fault!" If so, then the guilt you are carrying is false guilt, which manifests itself in various ways: striving, perfectionism, wanting to please others, being driven, and finding it difficult to accept love and forgive yourself. I believe God showed me this false-guilt-inducing enemy when I was at that conference in England. As that gentleman spoke to me, God took me back to that incident when I was only 20 months old. As I began to receive God's ministry through the man who was speaking to me, a very strange thing happened: I began to wave my arms around and dance. My friend who was ministering to me said, "There's that little boy who's been scalded, trying to shake off the pain."

That night the trauma and fear and destructive power of that incident left my life. God set me free and healed me from that trauma and fear and delivered me from the false guilt and shame that Satan had used to keep me from God's best for my life.

The purpose for my sharing Alastair Roy's story is that the Lord wants to meet with you today. Jesus can heal you in every area of hurt. He loves you just the way you are, but He loves you too much to leave you that way. Don't let the enemy cheat you out of what the Holy Spirit wants to do in your life.

How did that healing change my friend Alastair? In his own words, he has more peace. He is more at rest with himself and others. He's gentler and not as driven. The fears he once had are not what they were. When the Father's love comes into our lives, then these words become a personal reality: "There is no fear in love; but perfect love casts out fear, because fear involves torment. But he who fears has not been made perfect in love" (1 John 4:18, *NKJV*).

Sarcasm and Ridicule

Elaine was a member of my congregation. She was sarcastic, critical, opinionated and loud. Sometimes, though, I would catch her with her guard down and observe her in a most tender scene with someone who might need a caring touch or a kind and sympathetic word. *Ah, a cover-up*, I thought. And I soon discovered that was the case.

Elaine came from a very difficult family situation. Her father rarely spoke with her as she was growing up. She never once heard him say, "I love you," and she soon learned not to engage him in conversation. Her father's coldness and indifference wore away at his marriage until her mother and father divorced. Elaine was heartbroken. She blamed herself for the breakup of the family, a common reaction among children of divorce, as we saw with Alastair. Rather than cry all the time, however, Elaine quickly learned that the pain building up inside her could be expressed through sarcasm and rudeness toward others. This became her effective cover-up. But, as is the case with all situations involving cover-ups, the pain was still there, and it showed up in other ways and in other places. This became more and more evident to me as I noticed that she could never accept a compliment. She was critical and sarcastic with herself, just as she was with others.

Jesus said, "And ye shall know the truth, and the truth shall make you free" (John 8:32, *KJV*). When Elaine finally heard and understood this verse in the context of her situation, she came forward for prayer during a Cleansing Stream retreat and was wonderfully delivered from the spirit of self-rejection. She repented for having believed the lie that she was not worthy of God's love. She asked the Lord to forgive her for not fully accepting His Word and for behaving in hurtful ways toward others. She renounced the door that had been opened to the spirit of rejection by her words and behavior, and the yoke of bondage she had been under for so many years broke. Jesus set her free.

She then had to learn to walk in her freedom. Over time, she rooted out her old habits and replaced them with better ones. She soon began to practice the kindness toward others that she now felt toward herself.

Perfectionism

There is nothing wrong in wanting things to be done right. But what about those with whom this becomes a driving force—a compulsion that motivates every action? Perfectionist behavior is often characteristic of someone suffering from self-rejection.

My dad was a design engineer who liked to do things right— his blueprints were meticulous. Those who built the equipment he designed never had to be concerned about missing or flawed information. He didn't rush things but took the necessary time to complete a project so that he wouldn't have to redo it. This was not perfectionism; it was a desire to do things well. God loves excellence—just look at His creation. What perfection! The kind of negative perfectionism I am speaking about hinders rather than helps. It suffocates rather than breathes life into others, as we will see in the following examples.

Compulsively Clean

Susan was the ultimate perfectionist. She was also an angry woman. Everything had to be perfectly clean and tidy in her home. She railed at her husband constantly for any procrastination, real or imagined, and displayed great anger against what she considered his lackadaisical attitude. Susan was also frigid, and their marriage was in a heap of hurt. Yet to make sense of Susan's behavior, we need to understand her background.

Susan grew up in an abusive home. Her mother and father were alcoholics. She and her brother would hide from their father when he would regularly beat up their mother. As a result, their home was always a mess—there was no order, no stability. For obvious reasons, Susan had much pent-up anger and resentment, and she vowed that no one would ever hurt her like her parents had. She would control her life (and subsequently those with whom she was in relationship), and her house would never be messy.

As a married woman, however, she constantly lost control of herself, screaming at her husband when he failed to perform as she thought he should, manipulating and controlling him through her anger. She also believed that she was never good enough; she was driven by a spirit of self-rejection. The addiction to alcohol in Susan's parents was just one form of behavior that spun off from the iniquity. For Susan, the generational iniquity took root in her through the addictive behaviors of compulsive cleaning and anger.

At the writing of this book, Susan and her husband are becoming more aware of their issues and are working through their destructive behavior together.

Desperate for Affection

John grew up in a fairly decent home. The only problem was that his parents were so busy with their own lives that they rarely had time for him. The home was safe, yet their home life was without much affection. John never recalled receiving any compliments from his dad or hugs from his mother. He grew up feeling that he had to fight for every bit of affection he would receive.

Later in life, John ruined relationships with others because he often overpowered them with his own sense of need. People felt smothered and backed away from him. So John became a perfectionist because he thought, *If I do everything perfectly, then others won't reject me. It's because they see my flaws that they turn away from me.* Adding fuel to the fire was his driving desire to be loved and accepted for who he was. But in John's own eyes, he was never good enough. His thoughts were full of his own shortcomings and inadequacies.

The spirit of self-rejection was also driving him away from the love of God because, just as he could never get the approval of his earthly father, he believed that he could never receive God's approval.

Chapter 8

Anger and Rage

Anger and rage are another manifestation of self-rejection.
They can often be found in the heart of those who have experienced rejection in the form of abuse. All-consuming, anger and
rage eat away at the heart while driving the body to acts of vio-
lence and addiction. Such was the case with Laurey Thompson,
an awesome man of God who was healed of his anger and rage.

As a young boy, Laurey was placed for adoption and ended
up in a very abusive family. His adoptive father physically and
emotionally abused him until he was placed in foster care, where
he was also physically abused. All of this abusive treatment from
people who were supposed to love and care for him enforced the
lie that he didn't have any worth or value. Laurey didn't understand why he wasn't accepted, which resulted in self-rejection
and self-hatred. He was tormented with the anger, rage and vio-
lence that lived in his heart.

When he was old enough, he went into the military, during
which time he became an alcoholic and drug addict. His severe
sense of rejection resulted in his spending time in a mental hospital. After his release, he joined a motorcycle gang that provided what he thought were acceptance and worth. Eventually he
came to the place where he was so tormented by his anger and
rage that he no longer wanted to live. By that time he was home-
less, and the constant pain of rejection and self-hatred had completely shattered his life.

While riding his motorcycle one day, he passed a church and
noticed about 50 other motorcycles in the parking lot. He pulled
in and parked, walked inside and met Jesus as Savior in this

church that opened its doors to the rejected, broken, angry, abandoned and desperate. The people there ministered to him, and he began his relationship with Jesus—but not without obstacles.

By that time, Laurey was in his 40s. He soon met and married a woman from Alcoholics Anonymous, and they began their life together. They started attending a small church in Colorado, where they went through the Cleansing Stream seminar and met Jesus as their Deliverer and Healer.

At first this beaten-down man could not look anyone in the face. Instead he would stare at the floor when people spoke to him. The shame of rejection kept him from comfortably relating to others. However, when he was unconditionally welcomed by the pastor and the leadership in that church, his healing began. He now leads their intercessors team, and he and his wife are ministering healing and deliverance to Native Americans.

Nothing is impossible with God when His love is given through His Body, the Church.

The Many Forms of Rejection

Sense of Failure

Many of us suffer from the spirit of self-rejection after we have not experienced success in some particular endeavor. This is especially true if we have gone through the pain of a divorce. No one felt more like a failure than David, whose marriage fell apart despite his best efforts.

David was 29 when he and Sue got married. Marrying just three months before Dave entered law school brought enormous pressures in their relationship during the first three years of their marriage. But they had a common goal—getting Dave through law school—so they worked to keep their relationship frictions to a minimum. Both had been raised in active churches, but both had drifted away from God once they left home.

After law school, they began to grow farther apart. David was working hard as a junior lawyer at a big law firm, putting in lots of hours, and Sue was working hard at her own small business. They shared less and less in common as they spent less and less time together. Once headed in the wrong directions, they lacked the tools to get themselves turned around. Neither of them had relied on God when they started their marriage, and neither of them reached toward Him for help when their marriage was in trouble. Finally, they divorced. "Divorce"—such an easy word to speak, but such a painful experience for many. David's divorce was no exception.

It had been David's desire and expectation to have a successful marriage. His parents had a long, enduring marriage, and David felt that he had the gifts necessary to have a successful marriage. He was intelligent and motivated and was rapidly climbing the ladder of success. His abilities had always provided him with answers to every problem, solutions to every puzzle, a way out of every malaise. But now, as his marriage dissolved, he felt both rejected and dejected, especially knowing that Sue had been previously married to a physically and emotionally abusive husband—and that first marriage had lasted longer than David and Sue's. David came to the conclusion that he must have been a worse husband than the abusive one. Not only had he not been smart enough to make his marriage last, but he also found himself compared to a man who abused and beat his wife. In David's mind, *he* was now the lowest of the low.

David turned his back on pretty much everyone and everything other than his work. He was aching from the rejection he felt, but he built up a wall around his broken heart in an attempt to bury the pain and keep everyone away, including God. He moved into a small house by himself and spent even longer hours at work, trying to move up the ladder toward partnership at the law firm.

One day, while David was on his morning commute to work, God reached him through the radio. David had begun listening to Christian broadcasts when driving from suburban Glendora, California, to USC Law School. As he continued working in downtown Los Angeles, he also continued listening to these programs. God effectively used the teaching on these programs to chip away at the barrier David had put up against Him.

About three-and-a-half years after David and Sue separated, David had what he now realizes was a spiritual breakthrough regarding the idea that salvation is an unearned gift, available to us regardless of our belief. He realized that he did not have to *believe* in what Jesus had done for him before he *accepted* what He had done for him.

This breakthrough motivated him to go to church for the first time in many years. He went to hear Lloyd Ogilvie at Hollywood Presbyterian Church. It turned out to be the Sunday that Reverend Ogilvie announced his appointment as Chaplain of the United States Senate, informing the congregation that he would be leaving after the following Sunday.

David then decided to check out Pastor Jack Hayford's church in Van Nuys, and during David's very first service at Church On

The Way, he responded to the altar call. From then on he felt that God was speaking directly to his heart each and every time he attended. Every message was directly related to something he had been struggling with during the preceding week—or would face in the coming week.

David had always loved being around kids, so when he eventually joined Pastor Hayford's church, he volunteered to work in children's ministries. He started out working in the nursery because he thought the babies would accept whatever he had to give—which, at that point in his life, did not seem to be very much. God tenderly used those babies and all the kids in the church's children's ministries to begin to restore David's broken heart and draw him back to God.

While David held the babies who were crying and missing their moms and dads during church services, God poured His love through David's heart into those hurting children. By necessity, David had to open up his heart to God so that he would have something to give to those little ones. As the children gathered around him—sometimes three or four at a time—to be touched or held, David, in turn, would draw closer to God to be touched and held by Him.

David felt God's love and acceptance as the children accepted the love and affection he gave to them. As they were comforted, he was comforted by God. He learned the truth of Mark 9:37 (*NKJV*): "Whoever receives one of these little children in My name receives Me; and whoever receives Me, receives not Me but Him who sent Me." It took years, but this flow of God's love through David's heart not only touched the children he ministered to, but also restored and strengthened his own heart.

In time, David became involved with Cleansing Stream Ministries at the church, eventually serving as an intercessor at retreats. During a time of intercessory prayer, the team began singing the song "He Knows My Name"[1]—a song that David had sung many times with the children. The lyrics speak of the intimacy of God's love for us and that He knows each of us by name. As he sang, David felt as if God tapped him on the shoulder and said, "Who do you think chose your name?" The name "David" in Hebrew means "Beloved." God spoke to David's heart and said, "I chose your name and put it in your parents' heart so that whenever anyone called you by name, you would be reminded that you are My beloved and that your earthly parents loved you enough to tell the whole world of their love by calling you their beloved."

The tenderness of that moment in God's presence was overwhelming. What God said to David meant that He truly did know David while he was in his mother's womb and that He had been with him from the beginning. As God looked through the future into David's life, He knew that he would have difficulty feeling God's acceptance and love and that he would be hurt by rejection. And so God gave David his name so that he would know that God had always been with him and always would be with him; that He always had loved him and always would love him; that He would never leave him and never stop loving him, no matter how far he strayed from God.

Every day that David hears his name or writes his signature, he is reminded of God's love for him—how God came to be with him and how He is with him always. And every time he sings that song "He Knows My Name," David remembers that God not only *knows* his name but that He also *chose* it. This experience taught David that he is special, but not unique. He is special in that God has made him so by His extremely personal touch—in this instance of the name, and in many other instances. And yet he is not unique because God wants to give everyone a touch that is exactly as personal as David's. The heart of God purposes to bring all of us to the end of rejection.

Eating Disorders/Self-Mutilation

It is not uncommon to hear of those in bondage to the spirit of self-rejection responding to its pain through eating disorders and/or self-mutilation. Many who suffer from self-rejection cannot bear to see themselves in the mirror. When passing by stores, they avoid looking in the windows for fear of seeing their own reflection.

This was definitely true of a beautiful lady from Alabama, who was in her 40s and had been cutting herself and pouring acid on herself since she was 13. She had undergone multiple surgeries as a result of her self-abuse, and her doctor had told her that nothing would change her behavior and that she would eventually die from it. In desperation, she began to pursue a course of healing and deliverance, and she soon found herself attending a Cleansing Stream retreat with about 500 others who were being ministered to in the Alabama/Georgia region. Following this life-changing event, she told others that the Lord had met her there. She had been warmly embraced, loved and accepted over this two-day period. By the end of the weekend, her life had been transformed. God had delivered her from the spirit of self-rejection.

Seven months later, she wrote to the Cleansing Stream office, stating that she had not cut herself once during that time. Her pastor later confirmed her statement. Now, after one-and-a-half years, she is still walking in that freedom. God is amazing! His love and power are without limit.

Depression and Suicide

For those suffering from the spirit of self-rejection, depression and suicidal thoughts are not uncommon. They are the tell-tale signs of a life lived in bondage to rejection.

Jean DeHaven was a woman who was living under just such bondage. Her childhood had been a nightmare of abuse—she described it as "a prison camp." By the age of five she was planning to kill her family. By age seven she just wanted to kill herself. The suicidal feelings never went away, even when she was old enough to escape the abuse, and even when she found Christ as Savior.

She remained depressed, haunted by feelings of worthlessness, lonely and unable to trust. Then she attended a Cleansing Stream retreat, and this is what she said afterward: "I sat in the back corner, away from all the 'pure' folks, where I could keep an eye on everything." She went forward at the appropriate times for prayer, but there was no immediate life transformation for Jean.

"But God kept on working in me," she explained. "With successive Cleansing Stream sessions came increased understanding and increased trust. I am no longer suicidal, and I am no longer depressed."

In fact, Jean now says that she is so happy that when she's in church she just can't help rejoicing in worship with her hands held high. "A couple of people have told me to calm down a little, but I refuse. Isn't 50 years of depression enough?"

Jean had also struggled throughout her life with terrible nightmares. She knew that Psalm 127:2 gives the promise that God "grants sleep to those he loves," and she wished for that blissful rest for herself. So she followed the principles of repenting, renouncing and breaking. Soon the nightmares that had haunted her since childhood were banished, and she could finally rest.

"What Jesus has done in my life has been beyond imagination," Jean declares. "He has taken me from being suicidal to being overcoming and discerning. There is nothing He can't do if I cooperate with Him and have His kingdom as my goal."

Finding Deliverance

Jean is not alone. Countless numbers of people suffer with the spirit of self-rejection, but God's love knows no limits. Just as He delivered Jean, He can deliver you from this tormenting spirit—and like Jean, you'll find that there is nothing He can't do if you cooperate with Him.

But pride can hold us back from cooperating—from repenting from our part in allowing this spirit of self-rejection to have access to our life. So let's take a look at some of the ways that pride will argue, attempting to justify and compensate for the spirit of self-rejection.

- *"I am not that bad."* Pride tempts us to compare ourselves with others. "For we do not dare . . . compare ourselves with some who commend themselves. When they measure themselves by themselves, and compare themselves with themselves, they are not wise" (2 Cor. 10:12).

• *"Others have done far worse."* Pride tempts us to minimize our sin and condition. "There is a way that seems right to a man, but in the end it leads to death" (Prov. 16:25).

• *"There is no hope for me."* Pride tempts us to have a pity party while denying the clear statement of the Word of God that He is our hope. "May our Lord Jesus Christ himself and God our Father, who loved us and by his grace gave us eternal encouragement and good hope, encourage your hearts and strengthen you in every good deed and word" (2 Thess. 2:16-17).

• *"God can't forgive me."* Pride tempts us with false humility, which causes us to consider our weakness and failure as greater than the power of the blood of Jesus. "If we confess our sins, he is faithful and just and will forgive us our sins and purify us from all unrighteousness" (1 John 1:9).

• *"I hate what He has created."* Pride tempts us with unbelief, but if we deny His Word, we are left to our own opinion. "I will praise You, for I am fearfully and wonderfully made; marvelous are Your works, and that my soul knows very well. My frame was not hidden from You, when I was made in secret, and skillfully wrought in the lowest parts of the earth" (Ps. 139:14-15, *NKJV*).

Prayer of Repentance for the Spirit of Self-Rejection

Heavenly Father, I repent for rejecting myself. I repent for all the negative things I have thought and said about myself. I repent of not accepting myself, and for trying to be someone I was never meant to be. I repent for not believing that I have worth and value, just as I am.

I turn away from rejecting myself, and I renounce all the lies I have believed about myself. I renounce and break every curse I have thought or spoken about myself. I choose to accept myself. I break all ties with self-rejection and with every spirit that would lead me to reject myself. I rise up now against this wall of self-rejection, and I break it down in Jesus' name, amen.

Making It Personal

1. Was the topic of self-rejection a new and strange idea to you? Why or why not?

2. Did you relate to any of the methods of cover-up that you read about in this chapter? If so, which ones?

Have you used any of these methods (or other methods) to attempt a cover-up in your life?

3. Have you ever allowed pride to justify or compensate for the spirit of rejection? If so, in what ways? ("I am not that bad"; "God can't forgive me"; and so on.)

Note

1. Tommy Walker, "He Knows My Name," ©1996 Doulos Publishing (Admin. by Maranatha! Music). All rights reserved. International copyright secured. CCLI song #2151368.

FEAR OF REJECTION

And they heard the sound of the LORD God walking in the garden
in the cool of the day, and Adam and his wife hid themselves from the
presence of the LORD God among the trees of the garden.

GENESIS 3:8, *NKJV*

B ecause of shame and self-rejection, we try to hide from God and disguise who we are, hoping that both God and others will not see the real us. If we have experienced intense rejection, we will do almost anything to avoid the experience again. Shame is the result of self-rejection; self-rejection is the result of experiencing severe rejection from someone else.

Due to Shame

Adam and Eve tried to hide from God because of shame. This might seem ludicrous to us, for we know that no one can hide from God. Surely they must have realized that He would know where to find them. But when shame finds a place in us, we become convinced that any encounter with God will be negative. We often revert back to our childhood experience; if our earthly father rejected us, we tend to believe that our heavenly Father will also reject us. One of our adversary's main objectives is to convince us that God is not good—and not safe. The thought of facing Him in the condition of shame brings dread. We will do almost anything to avoid Him.

It's pretty amazing to see how God responded to Adam and Eve when they hid from Him. Their normal routine was to commune with Him in the cool of the day. The Lord certainly knew what Adam had done, yet He came to him in a familiar way, at the usual time. He didn't suddenly appear with fury, demanding an explanation. He came in the cool of the evening and called out to Adam.

> Then the man and his wife heard the sound of the LORD God as he was walking in the garden in the cool of the day, and they hid from the LORD God among the trees of the garden. But the LORD God called to the man, "Where are you?" (Gen. 3:8-9).

Some of us have perhaps seen an angry, red-faced parent shouting in frustration at one of his or her rebellious children, "Come here now!" Many of us imagine God doing the same with us. But God comes to us where we are—He comes to our hiding place. He condescends to our level for the purpose of reconciliation. The word "grace" means "to bend down." It is the picture of a king reaching down to a lowly servant. Nothing requires the king to do so. In the same way, our King bends down to us in love and grace to bring us back into a right relationship with Him.

The love of God can further be seen in His simple yet meaningful words to Adam and Eve: "Where are you?"

- Where are you?—"Adam and Eve, I desire for you to be with Me. You have run away from Me, and *I desire fellowship*."

- Where are you?—"It is My wish that you know and understand your place. You need to *consider what you have done* and come to grips with the choices you've made."

- Where are you?—"*You have value* to Me. If it were not true I would not bother attempting to find you."

- Where are you?—"I am giving you an opportunity to respond to My calling. You can choose to ignore Me, or you can *call to Me* of your own choice."

- Where are you?—"I am your God, and as such I have the means by which you can *return to Me*."

Due to Severe Rejection

God desires to rescue us not only from our shame but also from our sense of rejection. His love reaches into our hearts to bring wholeness and acceptance where once there was only brokenness and rejection.

I feel blessed that I have seen His healing at work in the hearts of the faithful. One particular believer's story has stayed with me over the years. Nikki attended our retreat in Colorado Springs and shared her story with me. What she had to say both broke my heart and inspired me.

Nikki hated herself. She believed she was worthless because all her life the actions of those around her communicated to her that she had no value. As a Vietnamese girl in the early 1970s, she had experienced firsthand the ravages of war. While still a little girl, her father had to escape his country or be arrested and most likely killed. After he fled, she and her mother never heard from him again. At the age of 12, she too attempted to flee the country. She managed to make it as far as Hong Kong, where she was rejected by their immigration department (though she was part Chinese) and deported back to Vietnam only to be sent to prison there. During her prison stay, she was raped by a guard. After six months, she was released. She then successfully escaped Vietnam and ultimately arrived in the United States, where she attended a church and gave her life to Jesus Christ as her Lord and Savior.

Yet Nikki was being tormented by spirits of self-rejection, abandonment, bitterness and abuse. A standard psychological approach through counseling might have had her in therapy for the rest of her adult years, but the power of God to heal the brokenhearted and bind up their wounds (see Pss. 34:18-19; 147:3; Isa. 61:1; Hos. 6:1) became evident to Nikki when, during a time of ministry at a Cleansing Stream retreat, we addressed the brokenness of abuse.

This is something we do regularly at our retreats, with a man standing before the women in attendance and ministering identificational repentance. This method is a means by which those who have experienced abuse in its many forms (physical, verbal, emotional, sexual or spiritual) experience someone who stands before them and repents for the wrongdoing. The "stand-in" begins by saying, "The likelihood of your abuser standing before you as I am now doing, and speaking the words I am going to speak, is doubtful. But I wish that person could stand here now as I am standing before you and say these words." He then goes on:

I am sorry for how I treated you. Perhaps I was your father—and I used my hands against you. I was rough with you and treated you harshly. Instead of my hands being a comfort to you, I used them to shove or hit you instead of protecting and blessing you. I may have spoken things to you that should never be spoken to a loving daughter such as yourself. You never heard the words, "I love you." Instead, you heard words such as, "You're stupid and no good. I'm ashamed to be your father. You are a failure and will never amount to anything. Get out of my life. Why couldn't you have been a son? I wish you had never been born." I should have spoken words to you such as, "I love you—you are so special to me. I am so proud to be your father. I will protect you as long as I have breath." You should have been able to sit on my lap as I hugged you and made you feel loved.

Perhaps I was that father who did a most despica-
ble thing and abused you sexually. I touched you in
ways that made you feel dirty and cheap. I confused you
and stirred up so many wrong feelings in you. In the
process, I made you feel that it was your fault. I am here
to say that it was not your fault. There was nothing
about you that made me do what I did to you. The
problem was me, not you. I made you feel dirty and
cheap, and now you have difficulty being intimate with
God. It is hard for you to trust anyone—let alone God.
How can you trust Father God when you could not
trust your earthly father? You want to be close to Him,
but once you attempt to do so, you begin to pull away.
I am so sorry for what I have done. And please remember that it was not your fault.

These and other words are spoken, both by a man to the men
and women, and by a woman to the women and men. One might
wonder how this can accomplish anything, but you would be
surprised. All their lives, those who have experienced abuse have
wished for their abuser to repent. And even though we are not
the ones who did the abusing, the fact that the words are spoken
brings much healing to these hurting men and women.

Afterward, we minister to them as God leads. We offer to
give them a father's or mother's hug. This is done by our ministry team. During this phase of our retreat, there are many,
many tears as those who have held the pain of abuse inside for
so many years are able to release their hurt and pain and have
the joy of a "mom" or "dad" giving them a much-wanted, tender

hug. Christians are meant to extend the love of God to others, and I can see no more perfect way in the face of such pain. The testimonies we hear from this time of ministry are astounding.

Of course, I would never minimize the trauma that those who have been severely abused have been through. During the course of ministry on this subject, we carefully take the participants through a thorough process of releasing their pain, anger and bitterness toward God, who is absolutely good, trustworthy and just. Releasing their "case" to Him who is the Supreme Judge of the universe brings them to a place where they no longer hold on to bitterness and judgment. It is only then that any one of us can receive true healing and deliverance.

It was during such a time that I learned of Nikki's story. She knew of my having been in Vietnam as a soldier in the Army. As I stood before her and heard her story, my heart went out to her. She shared the pain of having her father go away and how she wished she could feel her father's arms around her once again. As I stood in place of her father and gave her a tender father's hug, she wept and wept. I spoke the words to her that a loving father would want her to know: that he missed her and never wanted to hurt her or her mother; that she was a special treasure in God's sight and so loved by Him; that she was a special creation of God and had an eternal purpose in this life. The pain of abandonment and self-rejection was washed away, along with the deeply entrenched bitterness she had felt toward the prison guard. She released all her anger, pain and unforgiveness to God, knowing that He is perfectly good, just and trustworthy. God touched Nikki's heart in a profound and real way, and she was healed and delivered.

At the end of the retreat, Nikki did a most amazing thing—but one that gave evidence of her deliverance. She came up to me and said, "Pastor Hayward, thank you for serving in Vietnam. If it weren't for men and women like you, I would never have come to this country. I would never have known about Jesus. I would never have known the great love of God to set me free from the pain of my past."

God's love truly is amazing! Only He can set the prisoner free. Only He can heal the brokenhearted and bind up their wounds.

Changing Appearances

When we hate or dislike ourselves, we might attempt to become someone we are not. We might observe those who seem to be successful or who appear to have great approval from others, and try to copy them. There is a vast difference between superficially remaking your personality because of shame and attempting to be the best you can be by emulating the good qualities of those who have influenced your life.

In my own life, I often reflect upon the excellent example of how my dad modeled being a father and husband to us. Even after his going home to be with the Lord, his life continues to have a profound impact on mine. Perhaps you can think of those who have been role models to you. These godly people can be like beacons lighting the way, for they truly are gifts from God. Without these living examples, many of us would lose our footing and go astray. The apostle Paul once said, "Follow my example, as I follow the example of Christ" (1 Cor. 11:1).

If, however, we are looking for someone to emulate so that we can hide behind his or her personality and lose ourselves in the process, then there is something terribly wrong. Yet self-hatred drives us to do just that. Drawn to those whom we see as successful and loved by others, we begin to dress as they dress, speak as they speak and walk as they walk. In the process, we begin to lose our identity. We even find this behavior in the Church, as we watch some members become clones of others.

God does not want clones; He does not want self-loathing to drive hurt people to become carbon copies of other individuals. God loves variety—that is why He has created such a mix of personalities, talents and varying gifts from the Holy Spirit.

> Now there are different kinds of spiritual gifts, but it is the same Holy Spirit who is the source of them all. There are different kinds of service in the church, but it is the same Lord we are serving. There are different ways God works in our lives, but it is the same God who does the work through all of us (1 Cor. 12:4-6, *NLT*).

Though we know this amazing truth, that God loves us for who we are, it is difficult for us to break old habits, especially if we did not come from a loving home environment. Without parents who were able to create a loving, caring home with safe but firm boundaries, we, as children, were unlikely to establish positive identities. Most of our adult needs for deliverance were birthed in these early years of development, as we learned to hide from God and ourselves, attempting to be someone we're not.

This was definitely the case with Robert, a young man who attended one of our conference retreats. He walked in wearing a black trench coat down to his ankles. He also wore a black T-shirt, black jeans, black shoes, black earrings and had his hair dyed black. His Gothic look was, of course, a mask. I remember praying, "Lord, please help this young man. Help him to see truth, and most of all, help him to see Your love for him through us."

During the course of the retreat, I found out that Robert's father had taken off with his secretary and abandoned Robert when he was only seven years old. As Robert grew up, he felt cheated because he did not have a dad to come to his school plays and sports activities. Because Robert felt dead inside, he decided to wear the mask of death on the outside as well. If he scared people, then all the better—they'd leave him alone.

Robert's apparent indifference was just a mask to hide his overwhelming sense of rejection. It was actually a cry for attention. Through *our* love and acceptance, we began to demonstrate the love of *Jesus* to Robert. We didn't become indifferent or shocked by his behavior; instead, we spoke truth to him and respected and honored him in the way that we ministered to him. In time the trench coat came off, as well as the indifferent attitude. Within two days he was smiling and free of the demonic strongholds that had held him captive for so many years.

The Power of Love

Upon reflection, I have come to the conclusion that *love* is the primary reason why we witness breakthroughs. It is impossible to underestimate the impact that love has on those in need. If indeed rejection is at the root of every human malady, and rejection is the absence of love, then love is the key to conquering all that ails humankind. No greater demonstration of this truth can be seen than through the entrance of Jesus Christ into the human race. The Father sending His own Son to die upon the cross for lost humanity epitomizes the power and effectiveness of love.

> For God so loved the world that He gave His only begotten Son, that whoever believes in Him should not perish but have everlasting life (John 3:16, *NKJV*).

Certainly love was the key to reaching Jane, a woman who had experienced abuse at the hands of her spouse.

For the last 30 years, Jane's life had been a living nightmare. She and her husband, Bill, had begun their married life together with high hopes. Jane came from a loving and safe home, whereas Bill grew up with an angry father. Repeated beatings had left Bill scarred and rejected. His relationship with Jane was everything he had hoped for in a marriage. He had a loving and caring wife who accepted him as he was. Bill, however, expected too much. He looked for Jane to meet every need in his life, and in doing so he left God out of the picture. Jane was not up to the task of being God—she was not perfect, and Bill's growing demands to fulfill all his needs left her frustrated.

Bill began to be haunted again with the overpowering feelings of rejection. He was so fearful of being rejected that he began to drink just to anesthetize the pain. The more he drank, the worse the pain became. Soon he was an alcoholic. He was becoming just like his father—angry and abusive.

Jane was barely hanging on to her marriage when she and Bill came to Cleansing Stream for prayer. A team of trained people gathered together in an attempt to see Bill delivered from the tormenting spirits that held sway over his life. During the course of the evening, Bill found himself on the floor with four men attempting to contain him as explosive anger and pain began to manifest. The wretched price of a life of alcoholism and abuse was written upon his face.

His wife stood off to the side, an unemotional witness. The years of living with Bill and his problems had left her calloused and indifferent to his pain. Then something happened. As she looked at this tortured and writhing man on the floor, suddenly an ember of love was rekindled inside her. It was barely a spark, but it was enough to cause her to run to his side, brushing aside the others. She held her husband's head in her arms, placed her face next to his and whispered in his ear, "I love you." Miraculously, the belligerent behavior immediately stopped. He sighed deeply and then looked lovingly into her eyes.

The power of God's love, expressed through those three simple words by someone who had nothing left to give, had broken the demonic hold over Bill's life. In that single moment he was set free from alcoholism and anger. Such is the power of God's love when it flows through His people. And such is the deep human need to be loved. The kingdom of darkness simply cannot operate in an atmosphere of love.

"Behold, I Stand at the Door and Knock"

Despite our *knowing* that God's love can heal us and our wounds, we often fail to invite Him into our hearts to allow Him to bring about that healing. We are so locked up inside that when He comes knocking, we don't answer the door. If only we would remember that there is nothing to fear—that Jesus brings with Him only good things. "'For I know the plans I have for you,' declares the LORD, 'plans to prosper you . . . plans to give you hope and a future'" (Jer. 29:11).

Maria was no different from the rest of us—she had to overcome her fears when she heard the Lord knocking. Her life was changed because she allowed Him into her heart and home. But Maria had to go through a great deal to get to that point.

Maria had only vague memories of her older brother, Timmy, who died when she was just a toddler, though she still gets tears in her eyes and a lump in her throat when she comes across one of the few pictures she has of him. After his death, Maria became an only child; but by the time she was eight, she was very excited at the prospect of finally having a new sibling. Her mother was pregnant, but she was also quite ill. When both mother and baby died in childbirth, Maria was devastated. She cried almost constantly and clung to her father as if her very life depended on it.

And then he sent her away.

"I just can't take care of you," he told her. "I have to work, and you can't stay home alone." So he shipped her off to an aunt and uncle she had never met, a couple who had no children of their own. It didn't take Maria long to figure out why—they simply didn't like kids. And they certainly didn't want to be burdened with one that cried all the time. Within two months, Maria was shipped off again, this time to her maternal grandparents, who took her in and did the best they could to meet her physical needs. But they had no idea how to deal with her emotional brokenness.

Years passed, and little on the inside of Maria changed. At the age of 50, Maria was married and had 3 grown children and 2 small grandchildren, but she was as unhappy and insecure as ever. One evening, while she was home alone, she decided that life wasn't worth living. But before doing anything as drastic as committing suicide, she decided to give God a chance. If He loved her, then maybe—just maybe—she could go on.

Maria's oldest son, who had recently become a Christian—the first in the family—had given her a Bible. She went to her room and picked it up, letting the pages fall open. Immediately Revelation 3:20 seemed to jump out at her: "Behold, I stand at the door and knock. If anyone hears My voice and opens the door, I will come in to him" (*NKJV*).

And then the doorbell rang.

In addition to being unhappy and insecure, Maria had always been fearful of nearly everything, and she would never have opened the door when home alone, particularly after dark. But after reading the verse in Revelation, she knew that the person at the door was a messenger from God. She rushed to the front door and flung it open, and there were two men standing on her porch.

"We just came to tell you how much Jesus loves you," they announced, and Maria's heart leaped for joy as she ushered them inside. They explained that they had spent the day going door to door to tell people of Jesus' love—and had just decided to stop for the evening and go home when God's Spirit tapped them on the shoulder and said, "One more." At that moment, Maria knew that God's love for her was beyond anything she could ever have imagined or longed for.

"It was my year of jubilee," she said later, referring to the Old Testament command of God to Israel to "proclaim liberty throughout all the land to all its inhabitants" (Lev. 25:10) on the fiftieth year. "I lived for 50 years in bondage to fear and rejection, wanting only to be loved and accepted. And then God sent those men to my door to tell me how much Jesus loved me—just the way I was. At that very moment, God began to heal my broken heart."

As surely as God sent those men to tell Maria of His great love for her, so He now stands at the door of your heart—and mine—ready to come in and let His love bring hope and healing and liberty. All we have to do is invite Him in and then let Him begin His work of restoration.

Prayer of Repentance for the Fear of Rejection

Holy God, I repent for giving in to the fear of rejection. I repent of all lying and deception, suspicion and mistrust, control or manipulation that either I or my family have given place to. I repent of trying to please people instead of You, Lord, and I repent of my self-protective behavior and all self-pity.

And now, I renounce the fear of rejection and all the destructive behavior it has led me into. I renounce and break all soul ties and generational ties to the fear of rejection, and I break its hold in my life. I refuse to be bound to this fear any longer, and I break down this wall of the fear of rejection. I break it down now, in Jesus' mighty name, amen!

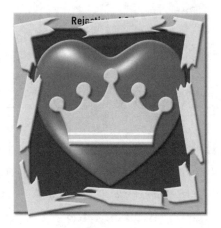

Making It Personal

1. The Bible says that "perfect love drives out fear" (1 John 4:18). How might that Scripture relate to the idea that God wants you to be free from the fear of rejection?

2. Are you holding on to bitterness toward someone who grievously hurt or abused you? If so, are you willing to give *your* case to God and allow Him to bring justice and goodness on your behalf?

3. Have you ever looked for someone you could copy or emulate? Why do you suppose you did that?

C H A P T E R   1 0

REJECTION OF OTHERS

Then the man said, "The woman you put here with me—she gave me some fruit
from the tree, and I ate it." And the LORD God said to the woman, "What is this
you have done?" And the woman said, "The serpent deceived me, and I ate."

GENESIS 3:12-13

Rejection of Others

When we find it impossible to rid ourselves of rejection, someone else usually pays. By blaming, faultfinding and pointing the finger at others, we are able to mask how terrible we feel on the inside and place our misery on other people. In essence, we reject them.

When I look at the Scriptures, I try to avoid making the characters so lofty that I can't identify with them. The prophets, disciples and other biblical characters were much like we are today. They had their weaknesses as well as their strengths, but often we make them superhuman and unapproachable. The Scriptures are filled, though, with ordinary people: "Elijah was a man just like us" (Jas. 5:17).

The Beginning of the Blame Game

Certainly in Adam and Eve we find biblical figures we can relate to. When they are approached by God to give an account of their behavior—once the cloud of sin had encompassed them—their reactions became much like ours today. Their immediate response was to justify themselves. Adam basically said, "Lord, it's Eve. Need I remind You that is was *You* who gave her to me? I wouldn't be in this mess if it weren't for her. She's to blame, not me. I'm just an innocent bystander. She handed the fruit to me. What was I to do—refuse it?" And Eve, standing there listening to Adam, excused herself by blaming the serpent: "The serpent deceived me, and I ate." (The devil made me do it!)

These two statements, though containing some fact, were not truthful. Truth requires full disclosure, and their disclosure was at best partial. I think that if we examine this situation, we can discover a more complete answer and perhaps find some insight into our own behavior.

Here are just a few points to consider about Adam and Eve.

- Their intellect was most likely greater than that of any human after them. Their bodies had not begun to collapse under the strain of sin. At the time of the Fall, they were perfect.

- No one had ever lied to them. All they'd ever known was truth and love. "Deception" and "hatred" were not even in their vocabulary.
- The temptation from the serpent may have taken place over a considerable amount of time.
- Eve could not understand why God would withhold something apparently good from her.
- She was tempted to believe a bad report about God.
- She was tempted to believe that she was of less value than a tree.
- She was tempted to believe that she could be more than human.
- She was tempted to believe that she would lose out if she failed to act and take matters into her own hands.
- Adam was fearful to confront Eve and prevent the taking of the fruit.
- Adam may have placed a higher value on Eve's regard for him than he did on God's.
- Eve was deceived; Adam was not. He knew exactly what he and Eve were doing.

Self-justification is just the beginning stage of rejecting others, but it opens the door to much more insidious actions. What God was expecting from Adam was truth that might have declared, "Lord, if anyone was at fault, it was me. I stood right next to Eve and did nothing. I watched her being deceived by the serpent and just stood by. I became afraid. I was fearful of what she would do if I were to stop her. I wasn't sure of what her response to me would be. Then, when she ate the fruit, I became fearful of losing her. I chose to accept the same fate as hers rather than risk being separated from her. In truth, I could have stopped it, but I didn't. And when she offered me the fruit, I also found it appealing and ate it, knowing full well what I was doing. I sinned, Lord, not only against You but against Eve as well. I have no excuse for what I did. In my fear, I ended up rejecting You—rejecting Your love, Your Word and Your ways."

Eve's confession could have been something like this: "Lord, I listened to a voice other than Yours. I had never been lied to before, but that doesn't excuse the fact that I succumbed to the deception. I know the truth of Your command, and I failed to obey it. I believed a bad report about You from the serpent. I began to believe that You no longer held me in high regard, and I resented it. I permitted the serpent to lie about You without challenging him. I also know the influence I have with Adam, and I used that influence to lure him into eating the fruit. I wanted the fruit and the knowledge it would give even more than I wanted to have fellowship with You. I felt that You had rejected me, and in response, I sinned against You and against Adam, rejecting You—rejecting Your love, Your Word and Your ways."

Instead of confessing the truth, Adam and Eve both responded by pointing the finger at someone else rather than taking full responsibility for their own actions.

How does this play out in our own lives today?

Spousal Wars

All of us have weaknesses. In marriage we know one another's flaws intimately and can easily point to them as a reason for our own failures. Owning up to our mistakes requires the kind of honesty into which only the mature will venture. More times than I'd like to admit, I have taken out my own sense of failure on my wife, Karen.

There are pressures in any job, and the ministry with which I am affiliated is no exception. At times I have struggled with everything that is involved in keeping a worldwide ministry up and running. If I fail to cast my cares upon the Lord, I can become frustrated and angry. This anger can spill onto my wife at the least provocation. She might simply question why I am making a certain decision, and I'll vent my anger on her by saying, "I don't need you to question everything I do," causing her to experience deep rejection. She has simply attempted to clarify and help, but since I have been questioning my own ability to make sound decisions, her question has inflamed my own sense of failure. So I have rejected her concern and input. The bottom line is this: If we fail to deal appropriately with our own sense of rejection, we'll only place it on others, giving further place to the spirit behind it.

Karen and I made a promise to one another before we were married. Whether it was her idea or mine (it was probably hers), I can't recall. We agreed that if ever either one of us said to the other that we wanted to pray together, this desire would not be refused. Now that sounds really good—unless you've just had a little tiff like the one I shared above. In the midst of that situation, Karen might say, "Can we pray together?" My carnal response would be, "No, we can't pray about it! *You* pray about it!" In other words, "*You're* the one with the problem. *You* talk to God about it." But we made a promise to each other. So now I say, "Okay, we can pray. Why don't you begin?" By the end of our prayer time, we are hugging and kissing. It is difficult to stay angry with someone you are praying with. And more often than not, the one who is angry has issues that require repentance and forgiveness.

If you are married, you might give this a try. You must, however, be fully committed to the promise. Otherwise you will end up playing the blame game.

It's very easy to blame those we feel may have caused, influenced or could have prevented our trouble. Difficult trials often spawn a sense of personal inadequacy. To accept that we might in some way be responsible for the dilemma can overwhelm us. So we look for someone at whom we can point a finger. Politicians on both sides of the aisle are especially good at this: If something good happens on my watch then I should get the credit; if something bad happens, it was the fault and responsibility of the previous administration.

There's an old saying: Eat the meat and throw out the bone. In other words, take responsibility (swallow the meat) for your own actions, and let go (throw out the bone) of those things over which you have no control. That's very good advice, not just for politicians but for all of us.

The Faultfinding Spirit

One of the names for Satan is the "accuser of the brethren," as we see in Revelation 12:10 (*NKJV*):

> Then I heard a loud voice saying in heaven, "Now salvation, and strength, and the kingdom of our God, and the power of His Christ have come, for the accuser of

our brethren, who accused them before our God day and night, has been cast down."

The faultfinding spirit partners with the spirit of rejection to frame a justification for its actions. It is not uncommon to find this spirit at work in almost every church. The door is opened to it by those who have succumbed to the spirit of rejection. Now, as they seek to find relief from the weight of rejection, they do so by pointing the finger at others, thereby embracing a faultfinding spirit. Eventually it becomes a pattern in their lives, and they become talebearers, backbiters and those who cause division. Unaware of their plight, they unwittingly become the agents of Satan himself as they follow his pattern and accuse the brethren day and night.

As a pastor, I found it interesting that those who have a fault-finding spirit are often, if not always, guilty of the very things of which they accuse others. You can observe this in the pastor who rails against the sin of fornication only to be caught in the act himself. This doesn't mean that any preaching against a particular sin means the preacher is guilty of the same, but it does mean that we who preach must constantly be open to the inspection of the Holy Spirit:

> And why do you look at the speck of sawdust in your brother's eye and pay no attention to the plank in your own eye? How can you say to your brother, "Brother, let me take the speck out of your eye," when you yourself fail to see the plank in your own eye? You hypocrite, first take the plank out of your eye, and then you will

see clearly to remove the speck from your brother's eye (Luke 6:41-42).

Many who fall into this trap believe that if they preach hard against a sin in which they are involved it will in some way even the scales. They will prove to themselves that they are fighting against that to which they have succumbed. For others it might be a matter of drawing away attention, for how could others suspect them of a sin of which they are so intolerant?

You, therefore, have no excuse, you who pass judgment on someone else, for at whatever point you judge the other, you are condemning yourself, because you who pass judgment do the same things. So when you, a mere man, pass judgment on them and yet do the same things, do you think you will escape God's judgment? (Rom. 2:1,3).

The unfortunate outcome of a faultfinding spirit is that this behavior always gains momentum, gathering others who will sympathize with the "righteous cause." There is a pattern to the behavior behind the rejection of others that is worthy of inspection. This is seen clearly in the story of King David and his son Absalom.

David and Absalom

In 2 Samuel 13—14, we read the story of how Amnon raped his brother Absalom's sister, Tamar. In revenge, Absalom killed

Amnon and then fled from his father, King David. Over time, the king was persuaded to allow Absalom to return to the kingdom, but under the condition that he was not permitted to see the face of his father. Eventually, however, Absalom was allowed into his father's presence; but by then too much bitterness had sprung up and too much time had passed—there was a definite rift between Absalom and David. With this unresolved bitterness feeding the spirit of rejection, Absalom plotted to take over his father's kingdom.

> After this it happened that Absalom provided himself with chariots and horses, and fifty men to run before him. Now Absalom would rise early and stand beside the way to the gate. So it was, whenever anyone who had a lawsuit came to the king for a decision, that Absalom would call to him and say, "What city are you from?" And he would say, "Your servant is from such and such a tribe of Israel." Then Absalom would say to him, "Look, your case is good and right; but there is no deputy of the king to hear you." Moreover Absalom would say, "Oh, that I were made judge in the land, and everyone who has any suit or cause would come to me; then I would give him justice." And so it was, whenever anyone came near him to bow down to him, that he would put out his hand and take him and kiss him. In this manner Absalom acted toward all Israel who came to the king for judgment. So Absalom stole the hearts of the men of Israel (15:1-6, *NKJV*).

This passage of Scripture reveals accompanying patterns of behavior in persons with a faultfinding spirit:

- A desire to present themselves from a position of strength
- A desire to show that they appreciate others' plight in not having someone stand up for them
- The planting of a seed of dissension by insinuating that they, if given a chance, would make better decisions than those in authority over them
- Rewarding with kindness those who acknowledge their wisdom
- Stealing the heart of others in order to gain support

I use this example because the divisions and schisms rampant in many churches often involve the rejection of others in concert with faultfinding. Consider the following story.

Pastor Bob did not accept or fully appreciate Ralph's idea about a design change in the proposed building project. As a result, Ralph became bitter. With this unresolved bitterness, he soon began to approach other leaders about Pastor Bob's lack of leadership. Ralph was often seen having these leaders to dinner at his home or taking them out to lunch in order to share his ideas. Ralph commiserated with these leaders over the fact that their ideas were rarely heard. He stated that if he were in charge, they would have a voice, and the right decisions would be made.

Soon the church experienced division—one group supported the pastor and the other supported Ralph. Ralph's group withheld their financial giving, and the building project failed. Finally Ralph's group left the church and began a new fellowship. Ralph's behavior reminds me of what we are warned against in Hebrews 12:15 (*NKJV*): "[look] carefully lest anyone fall short of the grace of God; lest any root of bitterness springing up cause trouble, and by this many become defiled."

"Falling short of the grace of God" does not mean that one has lost his or her salvation. "Falling short" means that we were once walking on the pathway of grace but are now "off course" or "off the pathway." If I am responding with grace to a difficult test (perhaps like Ralph, I'm not being listened to), then I will be forgiving and patient and will seek a better way to communicate my ideas. If, however, I fall short of grace, I will become bitter and unforgiving. The Bible says that when I fall short, I expose myself to a root of bitterness that will spring up and defile many. Let me share a story that illustrates how this can happen.

While pastoring in Texas, we had just settled into a new home. In the backyard was an ugly, sticky, gum-dropping tree, just two feet away from our house. I quickly determined that it was a worthless tree that needed to be cut down. Since it was only 20 feet tall and 6 inches in diameter, I felt that I could cut it down myself. Tying a rope to the top branch and anchoring it to the ground so that it wouldn't fall on the house, I took a saw and cut the tree close to the ground. I then cut up the trunk and used it as firewood during the winter.

Two weeks later, though, a new sprig grew straight up through the middle of the remaining stump. I was surprised, thinking that I had killed the tree, so I simply cut the new sprig. Surely that would take care of it. I was wrong. I had to cut the new sprig three more times before winter finally arrived and the new growth ceased.

At last I thought I had won. But when spring came, the tree sprouted again. Soon new sprigs appeared all over the yard—about 50 of them! A good friend convinced me that the root system of this tree had devised a plan to send up new sprigs from the roots themselves, thereby defiling the whole yard. I hadn't killed the roots of the tree; I had only dealt with what I could see on the surface. Once I destroyed the roots, the tree finally died.

In the same way, when we allow unresolved bitterness to thrive within our soul's root system, it has a way of impacting every area of our lives. It will sprout up in our future, affecting our family, workplace and ministry. When we give place to bitterness, it opens the door to faultfinding and rejection of others.

Racial Prejudice

No one refined the art of faultfinding better than the Nazis. Wanting to justify their warmongering, they implemented a plan to stir up public, focused, negative sentiments toward the Jews. Out of their hatred for the Jews, the Nazis created a propaganda machine to play the blame game for them. One of their spokesmen, Joseph Goebbels, wrote this famous essay, dated November 16, 1941.

> The historic responsibility of world Jewry for the outbreak and widening of this war has been proven so clearly that it does not need to be talked about any further. The Jews wanted war, and now they have it. But the Führer's prophecy of 30 January 1939 to the German Reichstag is also being fulfilled: If international finance Jewry should succeed in plunging the world into war

once again, the result will be not the Bolshevization of the world and thereby the victory of the Jews, rather the annihilation of the Jewish race in Europe.[1]

Media ploys such as this one effectively distracted the German people and much of the world from Hitler's primary goal: world domination.

The rejection of others can have far-reaching implications. Throughout the world, racial prejudice is responsible for the annihilation of millions. Whether we speak of Hitler, Stalin, Pol Pot or America's involvement in slavery, which ultimately brought about the Civil Rights Movement, their racist ideologies all have their roots in the rejection of others. By any measure, racial prejudice is satanic.

The spirit of rejecting others fosters ungodly pride. As a result, we begin to think of ourselves as being different—better than others. This pride is expressed in a variety of ways.

- Others are to blame for my condition.
- I would be successful if it weren't for them.
- My life is ruined because of them.
- If others will join me in carrying this offense, I can be justified.
- I'm not self-righteous; I really am better than they are.

Finding Freedom

If you desire to be rid of this spirit, then be honest before God and speak the following prayer from your heart. Remember, holding bitterness in your heart not only defiles your life but also negatively impacts those around you whom you love.

Prayer of Repentance for the Rejection of Others

Heavenly Father, I repent of rejecting others. I ask You to forgive me for all the hurt and pain I have caused them. I repent of my unforgiveness and resentment toward those who have hurt me. I repent of judging and criticizing them and for wanting to hurt them or tear them down.

Spirit of rejection, I renounce you. I renounce all the ways I have allowed you to influence me to reject others. I renounce all anger, unforgiveness, resentment and bitterness toward others. I renounce all soul ties and generational ties to the rejection of others. I choose to be a forgiving person, and I release forgiveness toward everyone who has hurt me. Spirit of rejection, I rise up against you, and I break down this wall of the rejection of others—I break it down now in Jesus' name.

Spirit of rejection, the blood of Jesus surrounds and engulfs you. You have no right; you have no authority to stay with me. I turn your sword against you. Rejection, I reject you! You are on a slippery mountain and have nothing to hang on to. I break all agreements with you. I reject your lies. The ground you have taken, I now take back. I reaffirm my trust in God and His Word, and I renounce every work of darkness associated with you. I sever all ties with you. I shut the door on you. You are exposed. In the name of Jesus, I cast you out of my life. Be gone! Let go! Now leave me, in the name of Jesus, amen!

Making It Personal

1. When have you been caught in negative situations, only to point a finger at someone else rather than accept the blame yourself? How did your reaction affect your relationships with the people involved?

2. Think of the people you know who seem to have a faultfinding or critical spirit. How have their attitudes affected your feelings toward them?

3. What might you do or say (or pray) to help repair or restore relationships that have been damaged by faultfinding and finger-pointing?

Note

1. Joseph Goebbels, quoted in *Das eherne Herz*, "Die Juden sind schuld!" (Munich: Zentralverlag der NSDAP, 1943), pp. 85-91.

PART FOUR

EPILOGUE

THE CLOTHING OF GOD

The LORD God made garments of skin for Adam
and his wife and clothed them.

GENESIS 3:21

How different everything seemed. The contented quietness of paradise had slipped through their fingers like sand. In its place came a frantic realization of the severity of their choice and its consequences. Sorrow seeped into their souls. They now had a reference for the previously enigmatic phrase "the knowledge of good and evil," and the agony of their grief was beyond words. They had lost their innocence.

Once something so valuable has been lost, can it ever be recovered? Can you go back in time and reverse the wrong that has taken place? Standing there in growing isolation, Adam and Eve longed to return to that fateful moment and turn away from the serpent, refuse the fruit, run into the arms of God. But they could do nothing. *Nothing.* God had pronounced the conditions of the Fall.

Reality was setting in. Even with the fig leaves covering them, they felt altogether naked before God and one another. But they could not hide; they knew of no place to which they could run. One day a distant descendant named David would declare,

"Turn to me and be gracious to me, for I am lonely and afflicted. The troubles of my heart have multiplied; free me from my anguish. Look upon my affliction and my distress and take away all my sins" (Ps. 25:16-18).

Though no words were recorded of their anguish, their cries of regret and despair rang so loudly that we still hear the echo in our souls today. The serpent, promising them a life without limitations, had lied. The sweetness from that forbidden fruit had quickly turned sour. And now, as they stood together, they knew they had failed themselves and each other. They could feel that something was missing from their relationship. And they felt the onslaught of death.

They were the first to feel the emotions that many of us now take for granted as part of life: fear, guilt, shame, condemnation, sorrow, weakness, failure, anger, bitterness, depression and deep regret. They had eaten from the Tree of the Knowledge of Good and Evil, and the serpent was right: They now knew something they had never known before. Indeed, their lives had taken on new dimensions. They had chosen their own destiny, unfettered by God-imposed restrictions. They now knew by experience what God had tried to protect them from. In a later time, God would speak through His servant Moses to repeat the instructions he had first made known to Adam and Eve:

> And now, Israel, what does the LORD your God require of you, but to fear the LORD your God, to walk in all His ways and to love Him, to serve the LORD your God with all your heart and with all your soul, and to keep the commandments of the LORD and His statutes which I

command you today *for your good*? (Deut. 10:12-13, *NKJV*, emphasis added).

Adam and Eve had succumbed to the most effective lie of the adversary: restrictions are unfair and unnecessary. If only they had welcomed the limitations.

Before Time Began

Before the time of angels and men, before there was a Garden on Earth, before Adam drew his first breath, the Plan had been set in motion. Man would need a Savior, and God Himself would play the lead role. He took full responsibility for His creation, and in the mind of God, humankind was unique and special. Only men and women had the capacity to know and love God. They alone could choose to love Him freely or deny Him completely. They alone could seek to know and obey Him, or turn away and disobey Him.

The risk was great. These special, created beings could turn away from Him entirely—and God knew they would. So in His fathomless love, God had already planned a way for men and women to return to Him. "But when the fullness of the time was come, God sent forth his Son, made of a woman" (Gal. 4:4, *KJV*).

Because of His great love, the Father would send His Son, unfettered by time and space, to become part of humanity. God Himself would pay the ultimate price, and it will take eternity for His beloved creation to know the full depth of His love. God would become one of His created, and he would do it through the agent of His Son. Jesus Christ would fulfill the law that humanity could not: "For the wages of sin is death; but the gift of God is eternal life through Jesus Christ our Lord" (Rom. 6:23, *KJV*). "Without the shedding of blood there is no forgiveness" (Heb. 9:22).

God's Son would pay for the sin that afflicted the fallen human race. He would shed His blood for His beloved. He would endure unspeakable agony on a wooden cross. The full weight of the sin of all who lived and would ever be born would be placed upon Him, who would then be nailed upon that tree. Once again, men would have to choose; they would need to receive by faith what only God could now do for them. This gift of God could not be earned or worked for; it could only be received with love and appreciation.

The concept of sacrifice was foreign to Adam and Eve. It would take several generations for them and their children to understand the fundamental truth that an innocent Savior would come and deliver them from the captivity of sin. For the time being, a picture would be worth a thousand words.

First Blood

From the beginning, Adam and Eve took care of all the living creatures, ensuring that harmony was maintained throughout creation. There was no fear among the creatures of Earth. Survival of the fittest was not the norm. This was a time when lions lay down with lambs—and blood had never been shed. Until now. Adam and Eve were certainly not prepared for what would happen next.

The lamb had been among them for several weeks. It had frolicked with the other lambs and cuddled with Eve during times of rest. How she loved this beautiful and playful creature! Now, as the Lord stood with them in the Garden, having pronounced the effects that sin would have upon them in the days to come, He picked up the precious lamb. For a moment, He stood there, gazing upon Adam and Eve with love in His eyes. Then came another look, one they had not seen before. It appeared that He was looking beyond them to a time yet to come. His eyes filled with tears and sadness came over Him.

He then took the little lamb, fell upon His knees and with one stroke, slit its throat. Unspeakable horror gripped Adam and Eve as the blood of this friendly, innocent lamb fell upon the ground. It attempted to cry out but there was no sound— only the look of terror in its eyes as life drained from its body.

How could God do such a thing? *Why* would He do such a thing? Adam and Eve stood motionless, paralyzed with grief and fear. They fell to the ground, staring in disbelief at what they saw. As the drama continued to unfold, the Lord cut the lamb open from head to tail. With His hands, He gutted and skinned it, and with the skins still warm from the blood that once flowed, He removed the fig leaves from Adam and Eve and covered them with the skin of the lamb. They were covered with innocence.

Return to Lasting Innocence

I have attempted to provide you with a visual picture of what Scripture simply states: "The LORD God made garments of skin for Adam and his wife and clothed them" (Gen. 3:21). Though my description is imagined, I believe it comes very close to the reality of what Adam and Eve experienced. I do know this much for certain: God was, from the beginning, providing a picture of things to come. He would send His Son as an innocent Savior to die a cruel death for the sake of His created.

And Jesus did come. He was born of a virgin, lived a sinless life, went to the cross and suffered great shame and physical anguish, died upon that cross, was buried in the tomb, and rose physically from the grave after three days and nights. By faith, if we believe and place our trust in His sacrifice for our sins, God will grant us the gift of eternal life:

> For God so loved the world that He gave His only begot-
> ten Son, that whoever believes in Him should not perish
> but have everlasting life (John 3:16, *NKJV*).

The word "gospel" properly translated means "good news." The good news is that the pain and agony of the Fall—the need to overcome our sadness, hopelessness and sense of failure—can all be remedied by fully receiving the gift of God's redemption through His Son, Jesus Christ.

Many, if not most, of you have already chosen Jesus Christ as Savior. But for those of you who have yet to make that choice, I want to provide an opportunity for you to do so. Here are the truths that, according to God's Word, we need to know and believe in order to be forgiven and redeemed. I believe that deep in your heart you are already aware of them because in each of us there is an empty place that can be filled only by coming into a personal relationship with God.

• *We have all sinned and broken God's law, and we all need a*
  Savior. "For all have sinned and fall short of the glory

of God" (Rom. 3:23). "Therefore, just as sin entered the world through one man, and death through sin, and in this way death came to all men, because all sinned" (5:12).

• *Sin has separated us from God.* "For the wages of sin is death" (Rom. 6:23).

• *God loves you and has made a way for you to be forgiven and restored to Him.* "Yet to all who received him, to those who believed in his name, he gave the right to become children of God" (John 1:12). "For God so loved the world that he gave his one and only Son, that whoever believes in him shall not perish but have eternal life" (3:16).

• *You can't earn salvation, but you may receive it as a gift from God.* "For the wages of sin is death, but *the gift of God is eternal life in Christ Jesus* our Lord" (Rom. 6:23, emphasis added). "For it is by grace you have been saved, through faith—and this not from yourselves, it is the gift of God—not by works, so that no one can boast" (Eph. 2:8-9).

I would now like to share my own testimony with you and, at the end, offer a suggested prayer—one that I prayed and through which I received forgiveness of my sins and came into a personal walk with Jesus Christ.

How My Own Fig Leaves Came Off

A sandbag makes a strange altar. Yet at that moment in Vietnam, a coarse, dusty bag suddenly became holy ground. For the first time in my life, I encountered the living God. I say living, for until that time I had created my own image of God. Now my life and my self-made god were falling apart.

It was a strange place for such a meeting. I sat motionless on a wall of sandbags that bordered the 504th Military Police Battalion just outside the city of Qui Nhon, Vietnam. It was monsoon season, 1967. As I sat there at 10 o'clock at night, it seemed my world was collapsing from within. I had done a lot of talking about God—but had certainly never really known Him. What had brought me to this strange place at this awful time, and how did I end up here—like this?

Two weeks earlier I had been in the home of a missionary, Paul Travis; he and his wife had been in Vietnam for more than 42 years. They had been through the Japanese occupation, the French occupation and now the American occupation of this small but strategic country. This godly couple had been instrumental in establishing a number of churches throughout the land. Mr. Travis was highly respected, and I was grossly ignorant, for even though I was a chaplain's assistant, I was very far away from God.

Since the age of 14, my life's ambition had been wrapped up in the occult—and I wanted to become a medium. Being fairly well versed in all matters related to the occult, I naively imagined that I could teach Mr. Travis, thinking he could learn from my vast experience and knowledge. While I sat on his counter and he cut vegetables in his little home in Qui Nhon, he somehow endured my endless nonsense for almost 30 minutes. He was getting a lesson on reincarnation, spiritism and the necessity of karma. I was teaching him all about the great teachers and thinkers of our time. Finally he'd had enough. He put down his knife, looked at me and said, "What a shame!"

Shocked, I replied, "What do you mean, 'What a shame'?"

He simply responded, "You don't believe in a personal God, do you?"

With his one simple remark, I was undone. No Scripture, no sermon—just one simple question.

For two weeks, his words rocked me. All my life I had been yearning to know God. I knew there had to be something or Someone. From this moment of reckoning, I felt like a bucket full of holes, and whatever I tried to fill it with quickly flowed out. There was no end to the possibilities because there were very few limits in my life. The security of feeling that I had everything figured out evaporated. My head and my heart were corrupt, and I was empty inside.

Now, sitting on that sandbag wall around the perimeter of the 504th Military Police Battalion, I was at the end of myself. Despite my extensive pursuit of spirituality, I had never before spoken with God. Prayer had been all about me, and I did the talking. Now God had something to say. And in the presence of His infinite holiness, a mirror was held up to my life. That mirror reflected all the ugliness there; what I thought was substance turned out to be a facade. My belief system was empty—it just wouldn't hold up under the strain of this real life.

God gave me a choice that night: I was invited to embrace His Son, Jesus Christ, or choose to forever walk the path I currently traveled. I recall running into the chapel tent, falling on my knees and crying out, "Jesus, Jesus!" At the time, that was the depth of my theological understanding. I needed Jesus, and

He came in. Then my Christian walk began.

Who had been praying for my salvation? I knew of no one. My parents certainly prayed for me. They prayed for health and a safe return but not for my salvation. It wouldn't be until some years later that I would discover the answer.

It was Karen, who later became my wife, who had been praying for me. When she was in the seventh grade, her Sunday School teacher asked all of the girls, "How many of you are praying for your husbands?" Of course, this question was met with giggles—they protested that they didn't even know who their husbands would be. The wise teacher answered, "That's true; you don't know—but God does. You should be praying for him every day."

Karen took her assignment quite seriously. From that moment on, every day of her life, she prayed for me. Then, two weeks into this new venture, the Lord spoke to her heart and said, "You're praying for him as if he knows Me. He doesn't!" At that point Karen began to pray, "Lord, make him miserable until he comes to know You." God answered her prayers. I was miserable and empty inside, and I knew of only one person who could fill this great void in my life. Up until that moment, I had vainly attempted to fill it myself, but like Adam and Eve eating the forbidden fruit, my attempts to fill the black hole in my life produced nothing more than an emptiness that could not be satisfied.

All my weaknesses, character deficiencies and sins became very clear to me on that monsoon evening in Vietnam. After I fell to my knees in the chapel, I surrendered to Him and to His Word, which declares, "And everyone who calls on the name of the Lord will be saved" (Acts 2:21).

Dear reader, if you have not already done so, I invite you, too, to fall on your knees, confess your sins and call on the name of the Lord.

> *Heavenly Father, I confess to You that my life apart from You is empty. I am spiritually lost and desperately need a Savior. I believe that Jesus died for my sins. I invite You into my life. Become my Lord and Savior. I surrender my life to You now. Please fill me with Your Spirit. I choose from this moment on to live for You. Please teach me Your ways. Thank You for the gift of eternal life. Amen.*

If you prayed this prayer, I invite you to contact me via the Cleansing Stream Ministries website. You can find the address listed in the back of this book.

Making It Personal

1. What was your reaction to the graphic description of God's sacrifice of the lamb to cover Adam's and Eve's nakedness with innocence?

2. Name all the comparisons you can think of between God's slaying of the innocent little lamb and the crucifixion of Jesus Christ.

EVIDENCE OF GRACE

And the LORD God said, "The man has now become like one of us, knowing good and evil. He must not be allowed to reach out his hand and take also from the tree of life and eat, and live forever." So the LORD God banished him from the Garden of Eden to work the ground from which he had been taken. After he drove the man out, he placed on the east side of the Garden of Eden cherubim and a flaming sword flashing back and forth to guard the way to the tree of life.

GENESIS 3:22-24

Many paintings have tried to capture the moment in history when God banished Adam and Eve from the Garden. Most have succeeded in displaying an angry God with His arm thrust out to the side, pointing the way out of the Garden. Yet the Scriptures don't warrant such a vision. God's motivation has always been love; He acts for the good of humanity—always. There is no reason to suggest anything else.

Adam and Eve had just witnessed the most terrifying sight of their lives: God's killing of an innocent animal and shedding its blood, then covering them with the animal's skin. Still reeling from that experience, they heard the declaration that they must depart from the Garden, lest they be tempted to eat the fruit of the Tree of Life. At one time they were invited to partake of its beautiful, life-giving fruit as much as they wished. Now it was forbidden. Wouldn't it seem good, having tasted of death, if they could now reverse the curse and eat of the Tree of Life once again?

But that simply was not possible.

The Ways of Death and Life

When Adam and Eve ate the forbidden fruit, death came in three ways: death to our spirit, death to our soul and death to our body.

Our Spirit

The Bible states that when we receive Jesus Christ as Lord and Savior, the Holy Spirit comes to take up residence within us: "The Spirit himself testifies with our spirit that we are God's children" (Rom. 8:16). Scripture also explains that before the Holy Spirit came to live in us, our human spirit was dead because of sin: "When you were dead in your sins and in the uncircumcision of your sinful nature, God made you alive with Christ. He forgave us all our sins" (Col. 2:13).

Our sins had cut us off from God. We had a fallen nature, which was inherited from our distant father, Adam. Jesus came so that He could impart to us the Holy Spirit who would stir our spirit to life again.

> Therefore, just as sin entered the world through one
> man, and death through sin, and in this way death came
> to all men, because all sinned. . . . But the gift is not like
> the trespass. For if the many died by the trespass of the
> one man, how much more did God's grace and the gift

that came by the grace of the one man, Jesus Christ, over-flow to the many! (Rom. 5:12,15).

Now, because our spirit is alive, we can communicate with God. We can have a relationship with Him that goes far beyond the ordinary. As His children, we can also hear His voice and be led by His Spirit. We can know Him intimately and understand truths that were hidden from us. We share in His nature and are regarded with tremendous blessing as joint-heirs with His Son, Jesus Christ.

> Now if we are children, then we are heirs—heirs of God and co-heirs with Christ, if indeed we share in his suf-ferings in order that we may also share in his glory (Rom. 8:17).

Our Soul

Mind, emotions and will—these three components comprise our soul. In a very real way, rejection impacts our soul more than anything else. Death and rejection are soulmates. They partner to bring human misery and pain. Death is the force, and rejec-tion is the outcome. When filled with rejection, we cease to think soundly; we embrace fear and make unsound choices.

Adam and Eve faced an uncertain future. Eve would know pain and unfulfilled expectations. Adam would know sweat and futility.

> To the woman He said: "I will greatly multiply your sor-row and your conception; in pain you shall bring forth

children; Your desire shall be for your husband, and he shall rule over you." Then to Adam He said, "Because you have heeded the voice of your wife, and have eaten from the tree of which I commanded you, saying, 'You shall not eat of it': Cursed is the ground for your sake; in toil you shall eat of it all the days of your life. Both thorns and thistles it shall bring forth for you, and you shall eat the herb of the field. In the sweat of your face you shall eat bread till you return to the ground, for out of it you were taken; for dust you are, and to dust you shall return" (Gen. 3:16-19, *NKJV*).

God's Plan includes restoring our soul, and that's what this book has largely addressed. Because of Jesus' sacrifice on the cross, we can find healing for our mind, will and emotions. God's power can drive out rejection and confusion, allowing us to receive the wholeness of His Spirit and grace. Our lives do not have to be subject to reckless, selfish living; we can, by His grace, learn to walk in wisdom and holiness in our thoughts, feelings and decisions.

Our Body

From the moment Adam and Eve took that first bite of forbidden fruit, their bodies began the process of deterioration. The Plan of the ages would set into motion the possibility for redemption. In the fullness of time, God would send His Son to die upon the cross. He was without sin, so the grave could not hold Him, and Death was conquered.

- O death, where is thy sting? O grave, where is thy victory? (1 Cor. 15:55, *KJV*).

- And God will wipe away every tear from their eyes; there shall be no more death, nor sorrow, nor crying. There shall be no more pain, for the former things have passed away (Rev. 21:4, *NKJV*).

And herein lies the dilemma. If Adam and Eve ate of the Tree of Life, they would forever be trapped in a body tainted by corruption. The Plan called for a new body—a resurrected body like that of Jesus, a body that would surpass the one in which they now dwelt.

In a flash, in the twinkling of an eye, at the last trumpet. For the trumpet will sound, the dead will be raised imperishable, and we will be changed. For the perishable must clothe itself with the imperishable, and the mortal with immortality. When the perishable has been clothed with the imperishable, and the mortal with immortality, then the saying that is written will come true: "Death has been swallowed up in victory" (1 Cor. 15:52-54).

The first evidence of grace was the redemptive clothing God gave them, clothing that declared they were covered with the righteousness of God. The second evidence of grace was God's pronouncement that sent Adam and Eve out of the Garden.

A Final Look at the Fall

Adam and Eve felt the pangs of regret with each step they took outside the Paradise they had called home. The weight of God's glory had given way to a world that was now under the weight of sin. Creation itself seemed to groan. The brilliant colors faded from the leaves and flowers; the once-fearless animals darted into holes or scurried up trees, echoing the loneliness Adam and Eve felt. They could not look at each other. Instead, they kept their eyes on the ground beneath their feet, watching their footprints lead them farther and farther away from the only home they had ever known.

Yet, even as they left, they were also reminded of God's great love and mercy. In that last face-to-face conversation in Eden, God had given them a promise that someday a Savior would come; in fact, they were clothed with that reminder. A distant hope stirred way down deep inside of them each time their hands brushed against the rough animal skin that clothed them: Another sacrifice would one day be made. A sinless Savior would someday come, and His power and glory would forever crush the head of the adversary.

> And I will put enmity between you and the woman, and between your offspring and hers; he will crush your head, and you will strike his heel (Gen. 3:15).

After hours of silent walking, Adam and Eve stopped. Falling exhausted upon a grassy field, they could still faintly see the light where the angel stood with flaming sword to guard the entrance to Eden. Was this real? Was this really their first night sleeping outside His glory-infused Garden? They lay there, unable to speak, their shallow breathing sounding empty and forlorn. Countless images and sounds ran through their minds: the fruit, the Fall, the fear, the hiding, the confrontation, the sacrifice, the judgment . . . and the promise. Mostly, their thoughts went to their loving Lord.

There was still hope. Their past was not their future. He had covered their shame and broken down the walls of rejection that separated them from His blessings. Though they and their descendents would have to live under the consequences of their rejection, they were not doomed to eternal separation from God. God was already at work restoring His fallen creation, and He would continue until it was finished. One thing they could declare to all future generations was the mercy and grace of God. And a seed had been planted that would ultimately bring about the utter destruction of their adversary and the end of rejection. God's Plan was unstoppable; His love was enduring. He would redeem humanity and welcome them once again into the Paradise of His presence.

This reminder of God's great love and faithfulness stirred something new within them. In the Garden they had praised God for His beauty and blessings; outside the Garden another stirring of worship began—praise based not upon their happy circumstances but born of a grateful heart that had been reconciled to a loving God who had redeemed them by blood. God's act of sacrifice had not fallen upon deaf ears and blind eyes. Adam and Eve knew without a doubt that some day the sacrifice of that innocent creature would become much more personal. They had seen that great promise in God's eyes—eyes that spoke equally of sadness, determination and joy. Yes, God would make the sacrifice personal by the giving of Himself. And that is where this new song of worship drew its inspiration.

Adam and Eve joined hands, and with tear-filled eyes they began to joyfully worship their God. They now knew what others would, in time, come to know: He would never leave or forsake them, and all was well because . . . *the Savior was coming!*

Making It Personal

1. How has reading this chapter (and the entire book) changed your own mental picture of God's sending Adam and Eve from the Garden?

2. How was God's sending Adam and Eve from the Garden an evidence of grace, as surely as was His sacrificing of the lamb?

CLEANSING STREAM
MINISTRIES

Please feel free to contact Cleansing Stream Ministries if you have questions about the resources, seminars and retreats mentioned in this book. Here's how you can reach us:

By Mail: Cleansing Stream Ministries
               P. O. Box 7076
               Van Nuys, CA 91409

By Phone: (800) 580-8190 (Toll-free within the
                      United States)
               (818) 678-6888 (Local)

By Fax: (888) 580-8199 (Toll-free within the
                      United States)
               (818) 678-6885 (Local)

Or website: www.cleansingstream.org

Pastor Chris Hayward's e-mail address is CHayward@cleansing stream.org. We look forward to hearing from you!

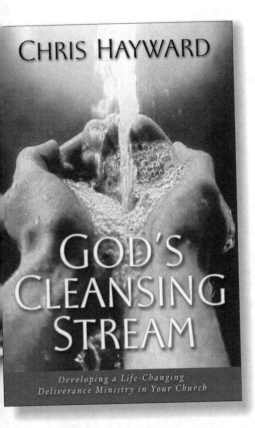

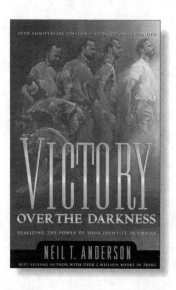
  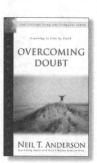 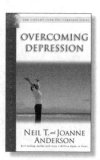